*The Way to Write
Science Fiction*

The Way to Write Science Fiction

BRIAN STABLEFORD

Elm Tree Books · London

ELM TREE BOOKS

Published by the Penguin Group
27 Wrights Lane, London W8 5TZ, England
Viking Penguin Inc, 40 West 23rd Street, New York, New York 10010, U.S.A.
Penguin Books Australia Ltd, Ringwood, Victoria, Australia
Penguin Books Canada Ltd, 2801 John Street, Markham, Ontario, Canada L3R 1B4
Penguin Books (N.Z.) Ltd, 182—190 Wairau Road, Auckland 10, New Zealand

Penguin Books Ltd, Registered Offices: Harmondsworth, Middlesex, England

First published in Great Britain 1989 by
Elm Tree Books

Copyright © 1989 by Brian Stableford

1 3 5 7 9 10 8 6 4 2

Conditions of sale for paperbacks:

British Library Cataloguing in Publication Data

Stableford, Brian, *1948*—
    The way to write science fiction. —
    (The Way to Write series).
    1. Science fiction in English. Composition.
    I. Title
    808.3'876

    ISBN 0-241-12662-2

Typeset by Pioneer, Perthshire
Printed in Great Britain by
Billing and Sons Ltd, Worcester.

For my son Leo
with the hope that he may find
something useful in it

Contents

An Autobiographical Preface

When I first submitted an outline of this book to the publisher the provisional list of contents did not include an autobiographical preface. My intention then was to write the book quite impersonally, addressing the various issues involved in the writing of sf stories in a fairly chatty but nevertheless objective manner. This seemed, at the planning stage, to be the proper way to write a book on the way to write sf.

I changed my mind because I found that whenever I tried to figure out what the beginning writer might like to know I found myself thinking about my own early days as a writer – about all the things I couldn't do, and all the things I had never even thought about. Then again, when it came to the business of trying to decide exactly what advice to give, I was continually forced to confront the question of whether my own writing actually conforms to the picture I wanted to paint of how to go about things. Convenience and honesty both encouraged me to tell you what I used to do when I was a beginning writer, and what I do now, as well as what I think *you* ought to do. Such personal testimony will, I hope, allow you to judge how seriously you need take the advice offered herein.

I wrote my first science fiction story in 1957, when I was nine years old. The characters went to the moon in a spaceship which the father of the family had built in his backyard; there they found a race of tiny humanoids brought to the brink of extinction by predatory dinosaurs, and saved them from this horrid fate.

Writing that story taught me two of the lessons which every writer has to learn. I learned how tremendously satisfying it can be to produce a story – to be able to hold it in your hand and think "I did that!" I also learned how dreadfully painful it can be when someone else, having been given the privilege of reading your work, tells you how unremarkable and silly it is. The poor opinion of another, whether expressed as a bad review or a rejection slip, is only marginally better than a poke in the eye with a sharp stick. The worst burdens of a writer's life are the injuries inflicted by rejection slips and the frustrations caused by those times when writer's block prevents you from working out what ought to happen next in your story.

It was, by coincidence, also in 1957 that I first made some money by writing. The *Manchester Evening News* had a children's section in its Saturday edition, where they would print poems sent in by readers, paying half-a-crown a time. I eventually reaped three half-crowns by virtue of stubborn persistence over three years. Every *professional* writer has to learn to keep plugging away. There are only two qualifications for being a writer: literacy and tenacity; tenacity is the rarer of the two.

I wrote my first novel, in collaboration with a schoolfriend named Craig Mackintosh, when I was fourteen. We completed a handwritten draft but never got round to typing it up, mostly because we couldn't type. That taught me two more lessons; first, that a novel contains an awful lot of words, but that if you keep on going you eventually accumulate enough of them; second, that a writer has to be able to use a typewriter. (I say "use a typewriter" because I never have learned to type properly; I got myself a typewriter and started picking out the letters with one finger. I am probably the fastest one-finger typist in the world by now.)

My schoolfriend and I wrote several more stories together, three of which were actually typed and submitted to science fiction magazines. We sold one in 1965 to *Science Fantasy* for the princely sum of £30. My share was worth a whole year's pocket money, and it convinced me that there was easy money to be made out of writing. Nowadays, it doesn't seem quite such easy money, because my expectations are rather different – I have to compare my writing income with my salary instead of my pocket money. The money you can get by selling a short story seems a lot if you only consider the time expended in producing that one story, but if you add in the time you invest in the ones which *don't* sell the situation looks very different. Between 1965 and 1970 I produced about fifty short stories; I sold four.

After a couple of false starts I completed my first solo novel in 1968. I had tried several times before, always setting off at a furious pace in the grip of fervent enthusiasm, but running completely out of steam after writing a few thousand words. I overcame this problem by deciding in advance that I must grit my teeth and subject myself to cruel self-discipline. I laid down a rigorous timetable for myself, deciding to start work at midnight every night for ten nights and not go to bed until I had written 5,000 words. I don't recommend this as an ideal way to write novels, but at the time it served its purpose: ten sessions at 5,000 words per session is 50,000 words, which would pass for a novel in those days.

Forcing myself to write showed me how easy it is to drift into a state of mind where you produce utter drivel. I found that there comes a point in the writing of every novel when you wonder whether it was worth starting. I also found that writing wound up my brain to the point where it was very difficult to get to sleep. Writing may not look like hard labour, but when you go at it hard you can get as high as a kite on your own adrenalin – which sometimes feels nice, but sometimes doesn't. Miraculously, that first completed novel – after a certain amount of revision to replace the worst of the drivel – actually sold.

Even at the time I was not under the illusion that my book had sold because I was a precocious genius. I had enough sense to be aware that the sf market was in a phase of rapid expansion, and that publishers were avid for new novels. I started churning them out as fast as I could (usually in four weeks flat, so that the task would fit neatly into a university vacation). I sold four more on the strength of my apparent promise before the publisher who bought them became impatient with my increasing idiosyncrasies. After three rejections I had to rethink my strategies of novel-writing and pay much more attention to making my work saleable. It was then that I first began to think seriously about many of the matters I will be discussing in these pages.

My failures also taught me how very precarious a living

writing provides, and encouraged me to keep other options open. I supported myself by writing for a few years, but when a decent job opportunity came up (by which time I had a wife and child) I took it. It was a good move, because the recession of the late 1970s interrupted the expansion of the sf market, especially in Britain, and selling became much more difficult. During the early 1980s I moved on to other kinds of writing, producing a great deal of non-fiction for reference books on sf and fantasy, and writing a couple of "futurology" books. That experience helped me a great deal when I came back to sf writing. Writing so much non-fiction about sf made me think much more carefully about what other writers had done, and how, and why – and gave me a much clearer idea of what I might try to do, and how I might go about it. The futurology books made me take the business of trying to build coherent and plausible images of the future much more seriously than I had in the early part of my career.

The above paragraphs are a rough sketch of the experiences on which I shall draw in my attempts to explain what goes into the writing of a good sf story and why. I shall try to indicate what kinds of imaginative skills the would-be sf writer must try to cultivate; I shall also try to point out what you can usually get away with while you are in the process of cultivating those skills and gradually learning to do things better.

I hope that if my teenage self had had a book of this kind to guide him, his writing would have improved more rapidly than it actually did. Maybe it wouldn't have – I am not entirely sure that his arrogance, ignorance and laziness would have allowed him to take much notice of advice which, I fear, often recommends hard work as the only sure way to improve. But I am reasonably certain that he would have been prepared to think about some of the issues raised here, and would have got some benefit from having a clearer idea of what it was that he was trying to do.

With those would-be writers who do not want to be told what to do, by me or anybody else, I have a certain amount of sympathy. If you are one of them, it will probably do you a lot of good to work out your own way of doing things, and you are right to believe that you cannot produce appetising stories simply by following recipes. But there is no harm in trying to think more deeply about what it is that you want to do, and what sort of problems you might have to solve in order to do it well. At the very least, a book of this sort should help you to do that.

I cannot promise that this book is a sure guide to literary success and fame. If I knew of any sure-fire method of achieving success and fame I would probably keep it to myself. It is sad fact that there is no way of writing which makes the job easy, and no way of going about things which guarantees that you will be able to sell what you have written. Mercifully, though, hard work usually brings rewards even when it does not result in immediate sales. The only way to get better at anything is by practising, and it is usually the case that the more practice you get, the better you become. I have derived a good deal of satisfaction and a certain amount of pleasure from my adventures as a science fiction writer, and I hope that this book might help others to obtain some satisfaction and pleasure of their own.

Chapter One

Science Fiction in the Literary Marketplace

The term "science fiction" was invented to describe the contents of those American pulp fiction magazines of the 1920s which offered extravagant tales of the future, featuring epic journeys in time and space, new inventions, and alien life-forms. Stories of a similar kind had been written much earlier, by such people as Jules Verne and H. G. Wells, but it was the pulp magazines which first set out to discover whether there were readers who would be interested in a regular supply of such imaginative fare. It turned out that there were – some of them sufficiently enthusiastic to become ardent fans, who would henceforth read nothing but sf.

In those days sf tended to be rather esoteric – the private domain of its fans. Because of its association with the pulp magazines, which were mostly devoted to colourful and melodramatic fiction with no literary pretensions, literary critics tended to look down on sf. Futuristic novels like *Brave New World* and *Nineteen Eighty-Four* were therefore considered by their writers, readers and admirers to be non-sf despite their nature. During the forties and fifties the number of specialist readers expanded, but it was not until the sixties that the ideas and conventions of the genre became familiar to a much wider audience. Nowadays there are very few people who have not read (or seen) a certain amount of sf, and though the market still relies on the loyalty of a hard core of specialist readers it is now possible for sf books to become best-sellers. Some literary critics still have not abandoned their hostility to the genre, but it is now admitted that some sf writers deserve to be taken seriously both as stylists and as writers with something interesting and important to say.

The expansion of the genre has been slightly unsteady. As a genre which existed mainly in magazines it suffered somewhat while the fiction magazines were being driven to extinction by competition from paperback books, but it eventually made the transition from one medium to the other and its writers found new commercial opportunities opening up as a result. Before the boom in sf paperbacks it had been almost impossible to make a living as an sf writer – Robert A. Heinlein, the first such specialist to become a full-time professional, depended for some years in the 1950s on income from books aimed at teenagers – but paperback sales made it possible for dozens of sf writers to make a decent living, and it is nowadays possible for people to contemplate making a career of sf writing.

Today, sf accounts for 5-10% of the new fiction published each year in Britain and America (it is impossible to be precise because of the problem of defining exactly what ought to count as sf). *Locus*, the sf newspaper, records that 298 new sf novels were published in the USA in 1987, along with 256 fantasy novels and 96 horror novels. The equivalent figures for Britain are approximately one third of those for the USA, the great majority being British editions of the same titles. Very few sf books are published *only* in Britain, and it is not necessarily the case that books by British writers are published in Britain first. It makes sense for writers working in the English language to consider the American and British markets as a single entity, and there have been several British sf writers (me included) who have published far more extensively in America than in Britain.

The nature of the sf market has changed dramatically in the last thirty years, mainly because of the decline of the magazines and the boom in paperbacks. At the end of the 1950s there were more than a dozen sf magazines in America and three in Britain, while paperback publishers were only just beginning to be interested in the genre. This meant that there was a heavy demand for short stories, which gave new writers abundant opportunities to break into print. Most of the famous writers who began their careers in sf's early days wrote a great many short stories, and even their early novels would be written for serialization in magazines without any immediate hope of a book sale.

Nowadays, by contrast, there are only three monthly sf magazines in America and a few which appear at longer intervals. Britain has only *Interzone*, which has survived for several years as a quarterly, though it will now be published six times a year and will be available for the first time from W. H. Smith's and other major magazine distributors. This relative dearth of short story markets has made it much harder for new writers to get started by selling short stories, and encourages them to move on as quickly as possible to longer works. In the present situation it is probably easier to sell a mediocre novel than a mediocre short story.

As the sf market has expanded the money which is there to be made by writers has increased very dramatically. Sf books began getting into the best-seller lists regularly in the 1970s. The first hundred thousand dollar advance for a sf book was paid to Robert Silverberg in 1978, and the first half-million dollar advance to Robert Heinlein in 1979. This means that sf writing can now be very rewarding indeed for its biggest names, while still offering the protection of a genre label to its newcomers. A book which is labelled sf will be attractive to regular readers of the genre even if it is by an unknown author, but the potential is now there for authors to break out of the genre straitjacket and go on to fame and fortune.

The sf audience has certain peculiar features. There are, of course, a great many people who read the occasional sf book as part of a varied literary diet, but there still remains a hard core of loyal readers who read very little except sf, and who tend to read a great deal of it. Although they are not particularly numerous these avid fans are an important force in the marketplace because of the number of books they read. It seems that the majority of these readers are young, typically becoming interested in the genre in their early teens. It is not unusual for them to become so involved with the genre that their reading habit resembles a kind of addiction.

Those readers who maintain their addiction beyond their twenties are most likely to be professionally involved in some way with science or technology—rumour has it that in large computer companies or the science departments of universities most people read no fiction at all, while most of the rest read nothing but sf. For many readers, though, addiction to sf is simply a phase which they go through, and although they may not give it up entirely the amount which they consume falls dramatically.

Market research carried out by sf magazines before 1970 consistently demonstrated that 90% of habitual readers were male, but that situation seems to have altered in recent times. Well over half of the new sf writers who made a name for themselves in the seventies were female, and many more females can now be found among the ranks of addicted readers, although there may still be significant differences between the *kinds* of sf usually favoured by readers of different sexes. We live in a society which encourages girls and boys to interest themselves in different things, and science and technology are still considered by many to be a male preserve. For this reason "hard sf"—sf which is most concerned with careful and detailed scientific speculation and invented technology — still has a large majority of male readers, while most female readers seem to favour "softer" sf, which pays more attention to alternative societies and exotic environments than it does to physical science and imaginary hardware.

Twenty years ago the sf market had to rely very heavily on the hard core of avid fans, because readers not familiar with the genre often found sf stories confusing and difficult to read. It was not so much that readers of sf needed to be scientifically literate, but that they had to become accustomed to sf's own jargon and the conventions of its narratives. Since then, science fiction on television has played a vitally important role in familiarising a much larger audience with the basic ideas and narrative tricks which writers in the genre habitually use. Programmes like *Doctor Who* and *Star Trek* have introduced an entire modern generation to the elementary themes and formulas of sf. This means that understanding what is going on in a sf story is no longer a problem for most readers, and that anyone ambitious to be a writer of such stories knows more-or-less what is involved. It is still true, though, that most successful writers of sf have read widely within the genre, and have familiarised themselves much more closely than

4

the casual reader with the vocabulary of ideas which sf built up.

The sf genre overlaps other genres which tend to be marketed under the labels "fantasy" and "horror". There seems to be a considerable number of sf readers who are equally interested in the overlapping genres. The relationship between sf and fantasy is particularly close, as one can see by looking at the way books are sorted by bookshops: the sf and fantasy books are very often mixed in together, with horror close by, but nevertheless separate. Many writers work in more than one genre, and it is noteworthy that some writers whose sf is at the hard end of the spectrum are perfectly happy to produce pure fantasy when the mood takes them.

Fantasy as a publishing category hardly existed before 1965, though there was a famous fantasy pulp magazine in the forties called *Unknown Worlds*, which was a companion to the best of the sf pulps, *Astounding Science Fiction*, and featured many of the same contributors. New interest among readers and writers was awakened by the astonishing success of paperback editions of J. R. R. Tolkien's trilogy *The Lord of the Rings*, which has spawned countless imitations and works in a similar vein.

Most of the novels written for publication under the fantasy label are set in imaginary worlds which resemble periods of our own past save for the fact that magic works. Such worlds – Tolkien called them "Secondary Worlds" in a famous essay – are often assumed to lie "parallel" to our own world, so that characters can move back and forth, as they do, for instance, in C. S. Lewis' Narnia books. Equally often, though, the magical world of the story simply exists instead of our world.

The fundamental assumption of fantasy stories – that magic works – appears to be in sharp contrast to the fundamental assumptions of sf, which is supposed to be responsible to the limits of scientific possibility. In a way, therefore, sf and fantasy are mutually exclusive genres which cannot overlap – but in fact there always has been a good deal of sf where magical powers are disguised as telepathy, precognition, psychokinesis and other paranormal phenomena. Sf has always featured imaginary worlds whose inhabitants are credited with such powers, and some sf stories set on other planets are hardly distinguishable from Tolkienesque fantasies, save for the fact that they use a different jargon to justify the superhuman abilities which the characters have. Many female sf writers have been prominent in developing this kind of sf/fantasy hybrid; Marion Zimmer Bradley's Darkover books and Anne McCaffrey's Pern novels are notable examples.

Horror fiction is distinguished as a genre not by its vocabulary of ideas but by the effect which it aspires to produce in the reader. It borrows its instruments from both fantasy and sf, and in recent times such traditional monsters as vampires, werewolves and ghosts have become so familiar that horror writers have increasingly leaned toward sf in order to discover new blood-curdling ideas. Horrible monsters and strange plagues frequently escape from laboratories in modern horror fiction, and experiments in medical science regularly turn out to have repulsive and terrifying consequences.

Horror, like fantasy, has undergone a recent renaissance, aided by the cinematic special effects which make the supernatural much more believable on film and which have helped readers to bring a more powerful and more vivid visual imagination to their consumption of printed texts. The relaxation of formal and informal censorship has also helped horror writers by allowing them to plumb new depths of bad taste in their ceaseless struggle to devise disgusting ways for people to be killed and mutilated.

Purists among science fiction fans often argue that it is easier to write effective fantasy or horror than good sf, because the fantastic events in these other genres tend to be stereotyped and do not have to be submitted to the rigours of logical analysis and scientific plausibility. Such claims have some substance, but are not entirely justified. The best fantasies and the best horror stories observe their own standards of logic and plausibility, and it is sadly true that a good deal of science fiction uses unoriginal ideas, displayed in stereotyped plots which pay only the merest lip service to the limits of scientific possibility. Fantasy writers have recently begun to strike back at such criticism by describing a sub-genre of "hard fantasy" which is richly and carefully detailed, set in conscientiously researched eras of the historical past which differ from ours only in the assumed workability of magic, and where the particular magic to be employed must be responsibly derived from anthropological sources. This has resulted in a certain overlap between the fantasy genre and the genre of historical fiction, though it is not yet clear how many readers will widen their tastes to take in both.

This book is addressed primarily to would-be sf writers, but many of the issues it will deal with apply equally well to fantasy writers, and some of them to horror writers too. There are good reasons, in marketing terms, for writers to experiment with more than one genre, and I will try to indicate points which become more relevant when writers move towards or cross these genre boundaries.

Because the population of the USA is three times as large as the population of Britain, commercial success in the literary marketplace is heavily dependent on American sales. American publishers produce more titles, and pay larger advances. Any moderately successful book will appear on both sides of the Atlantic, but it is generally more profitable to sell only in America than only in Britain.

The logic of the situation is such that when British publishers run into financial difficulties – as they invariably do in times of rapid inflation, or when overproduction of titles in a boom leads to a subsequent collapse – they can always play safe by not publishing any original titles of their own, simply reprinting books which have already proved themselves successful in America. This means that when times are hard they are doubly hard for British writers, and this is especially true of genres like sf and fantasy. There can be exceptions, though – during the last lean period, which lasted from 1980 to 1986 there was a localised boom in horror fiction in Britain, which allowed a few horror writers to thrive while sf and fantasy writers found their incomes in decline.

At present the British market is in an expanding phase, with publishers introducing new sf and fantasy lines or revitalising lines which had been moribund for some years. How long this phase will last it is impossible to say, but the prospects for new writers to get a toehold in the British market are probably better now than they have been since the golden days of the early seventies. A writer who can produce a promising novel can be sure of reasonably sympathetic attention from any of half a dozen editors. Even the short story market is looking more open, with 1988 seeing the bimonthly *Interzone*, the launch of the new horror/fantasy magazine *Fear*, and various publishers experimenting with anthologies of new sf and fantasy stories.

This combination of factors has opened up some good opportunities for beginning writers. If you want to have a go at writing sf you should strike while the market is hot, because it will be far more difficult to get in a blow when it cools down again. In the course of the next five years solid reputations will be made and spectacular successes will be scored. Very few new British writers have managed to establish themselves within the last ten years, but the next ten years will be different. The bandwagon is rolling, and anyone who is good enough, and prepared to put in the requisite work, ought to be able to jump aboard.

Chapter Two

The Distinctiveness of Science Fiction

This series of books already includes *The Way to Write Novels* and *The Way to Write Short Stories*. Some readers may therefore wonder why we need a different one to offer advice on the writing of science fiction novels and short stories. The reason is that in addition to the general problems which arise in any kind of fiction writing sf poses some problems which are uniquely its own. In this chapter, therefore, I want to discuss the special features of sf stories, and why those special features generate their own problems for the writer.

What qualifies a story as sf is that it is set in a world which is deliberately altered. Sometimes the alteration in question happens while the story is in progress, so that the narrative begins in a mundane setting which is then transformed by a new discovery in science or by some kind of catastrophe. Other stories precipitate the reader straight into a different world: our world as it may have become in the future, or an alien planet orbiting some other sun. There are also sf stories which feature "alternative histories", attempting to describe the world as it might have become if some historical event had happened differently – if, for instance, Hitler had triumphed in World War II.

Working out how our world might change in the future, or what life might be like on another planet, poses a challenging exercise in logic and inventiveness. Good sf writers attempt to make all the changes coherent, so that they fit into a sensible pattern. This worldmaking can be treated as a kind of game, and it has its own special charm in much the same way that a detective story considered as a kind of puzzle has a special charm. Part of the satisfaction involved in reading and writing science fiction comes from following the chains of argument which persuade you that if *this* has changed, then *that* must change too, and there is a good deal of pleasure to be gained from the display of non-obvious connections.

These chains of connection are perhaps best displayed in alternative history stories. There are a few such stories which begin by assuming that the Reformation never happened, and try to calculate what today's world would be like had the Catholic Church retained its monopoly of faith. They go on to argue that without the relative freedom of thought which Protestantism allowed, technological development would have been drastically slowed down, that the British would never have had the chance to overtake the Spanish and the Portuguese in the business of empire-building, and so on, and so on.

The construction of alternative histories also provides examples of how one can easily go wrong if one is not careful enough in making sure that all the changes are coherent. My novel *The Empire of Fear* is set in a version of the seventeenth century in which America has not yet been discovered. I was careful to avoid all reference to potatoes and tobacco, but I very nearly slipped up by allowing one of my characters to take quinine – mercifully, I looked it up in the encyclopedia in order to make sure that quinine had been discovered in the seventeenth century, and thus found out that he couldn't have it, because it comes from a South American tree. Readers who like the game-playing aspect of sf delight in catching writers out on such points, though the majority probably would not notice or care very much about such a minor matter of detail.

One of the standard exercises used in sf writing workshops is to require the writers to set a story in a world which is like ours in every respect but one. The stories written in response demonstrate readily enough how the effects of one small change can spread out to alter all kinds of social institutions, transforming the way we live; when exposed to criticism they also demonstrate how easy it is for writers to overlook or miscalculate some of the logical consequences of the changes which they have made.

Sometimes the fact that one change can have many consequences proves very productive for writers who can continue exploring the consequences of their inventions in story after story. Isaac Asimov's robot stories, which develop from his painstaking exploration of the implications of the three laws of robotics, provide an excellent example of how sf stories can be used to probe further and further into the possibilities opened up by one idea. They also show how later thinking can sometimes contradict earlier assumptions, so that we find Asimov in *The Robots of Dawn* suggesting that some of the earlier stories in the series have to be regarded as "fantasies" rather than bits of "history".

Because sf writing involves changing the world, the actual change which is made becomes the "focal point" of the story. Mundane fiction tends to take the world in which its stories are set for granted, and the focal point of such a story tends to be a particular character or a specific incident. Even when a non-sf story is set in exotic surroundings, or in the past, so that the characters may be observing different customs and mores, the writer is not inventing a new world, but simply re-creating a strange one. The merit of such fictions tends to lie entirely in the creation of believable characters and in the description of interesting incidents. While it is greatly to the advantage of the sf writers if they too can create believable characters and interesting incidents, the real heart of a sf story is the way in which the imaginary world has been set up to be different from the world of the reader. Kingsley Amis, in his book *New Maps of Hell*, makes this point by arguing that the real "hero" of a sf story is not a character but an idea.

It is the ideas in science fiction which initially attract most readers, and it is a hunger for intriguing ideas which turns many teenagers into addicts of the genre. To rush headlong through a vast series of changed worlds can be wonderfully stimulating to the imagination; the real world is moved into a new context, where it ceases to be the be-all and end-all of experience, but takes up instead a specific location in a grand scheme of pasts and presents that might have been and futures possibly to come. This enriches our mental life by making us sensitive to what might be as well as what is.

The fact that the focal point of a sf story is the way that it has changed the world has both advantages and disadvantages for writers. The main advantage is that writers who are good at the game of working out the consequences of small changes may be able to generate plots very easily. The extrapolation of an idea may in fact *be* the plot of a sf story, because it may be sufficient simply to watch the characters following through the logical consequences of having a new invention at their disposal, or working out some kind of puzzle which confronts them. A writer who can think of a few non-obvious consequences of a basic hypothesis can usually surprise the reader with a clever twist.

Thus, for instance, H. G. Wells had only to think of the idea that alien beings might arrive to colonise Earth, exterminating human beings just as Europeans had wiped out the Tasmanians, to have the plot of *The War of the Worlds*; the story is a description of the unfolding event. Then, the possibility that the invading Martians might have no immunity to Earthly bacteria (just as the Amerindians had no immunity to viruses imported by European colonists after 1492) provided him with a neat climax.

The chief disadvantage of the dependence on sf of its ideas is that all the easiest and best ideas were discovered very quickly, and once they had been discovered were partly devalued for later writers. There have, of course, been many other alien invasion stories written since *The War of the Worlds*, but writers who want to make use of the notion nowadays are required to find some new approach to it which will make their versions seem unusual. Should any such writer be so unwise as to conclude with the revelation that the invaders are not immune to Earthly bacteria, very few readers would be startled, and most would feel disappointed, or even cheated.

This makes things particularly awkward for the beginning writer, who simply will not know everything that has been done before. You may innocently happen upon an idea which seems surprising and exciting to you, only to be told after finishing your version of it that it has been done to death by earlier writers.

There do seem to be some ideas which occur spontaneously to very many would-be sf writers. The most common one of all is the story of a cosmic disaster from which only two characters escape, which leads up to the climactic revelation that they are Adam and Eve. Stories of this general kind, which use sf plots to reinterpret and "explain" events described in the Bible, have been dubbed "Shaggy God stories" by Brian Aldiss, and they crop up with amazing regularity in the slush piles of the magazines. Julie Davis, who was then editor of the magazine *Science Fiction Monthly*, once told me that about a quarter of submissions from new writers fell into this category. (The mesmeric fascination of the theme can also be judged by the fact that people like Immanuel Velikovsky and Erich von Däniken have written best-selling books asserting that all the Biblical miracles really *were* sciencefictional incidents!)

In one sense this is a problem which gets steadily worse as time goes by. As more and more sf is written, new ideas get harder and harder to find; no matter how ingenious you are, you will usually find that some clever swine has beaten you to it. This happens to readers, too, and is responsible for the fact that addiction to sf is often a temporary phenomenon. Readers who begin to devour sf at the age of thirteen will find something new and exciting in every story, but seven years and a thousand stories later they may well begin to feel that it all seems rather familiar. It is very common to find long-time readers lamenting that the Golden Age of Science Fiction is past, and that the genre has lost its vitality – but their idea of when the Golden Age was usually corresponds exactly to the first few years of their addiction.

There is, however, no need for the beginning writer to despair. Ideas do indeed get used again, and there is a sense in which they never get *used up*. There is always one more logical consequence which can provide a hook on which to hang a story. The fact that changing *one* thing about the world can have very widespread effects means that there are usually large numbers of potential story-characters whose lives have been affected in unique ways because of their particular circumstances or their particular ambitions.

One of the classic exercises in developing a deceptively-simple idea can be found in Bob Shaw's book *Other Days, Other Eyes*, which examines how the world might be altered by "slow glass" – glass which transmits light very slowly, so that when you look through a window you see what was on the other side of it years before. The book demonstrates in its conclusion that this apparently-trivial invention has the potential for unexpectedly dramatically changes, but it also shows *en route* how the lives of certain individuals are altered in different ways. There is a judge who must give a verdict now, knowing that a sheet of slow glass which "witnessed" the crime will reveal whether or not he is right in several years' time; a man who realises why his experiments with the glass have produced puzzling results, too late to save his wife from being blinded; and a man whose wife and child have been killed, but who can still see them at work and at play through the slow glass windows of his home. The would-be sf writer can benefit from studying this kind of book carefully, to see how one idea can generate a potentially infinite series of stories.

Other Days, Other Eyes also serves as a reminder that though an idea is the focal point of a sf story, it does not necessarily throw up the story automatically. Although some stories – like *The War of the Worlds* – do spring ready-plotted from the simple extrapolation of the idea, most do not. Many novice sf writers, carried away by the excitement of new ideas, put all their energies into the search for them, and invest too little effort into the matter of deciding what specific situation will best display the idea. Bob Shaw has said that the idea of slow glass occurred to him years before he figured out the one story which seemed to him to display it most poignantly (the story was "Light of Other Days", which is incorporated into *Other Days, Other Eyes*).

If your idea is a new kind of invention it *might* be that the best story you can tell is the story of how it is built and first put to use, but you must also consider whether it might instead be better to show a world which has already been transformed by the invention, and look for particular individuals who have found or been thrust into interesting situations as a result.

One often-quoted rule of thumb which may help in deciding what kind of story can make the best use of a specific change in the world is to ask: "Who will get hurt?" If you can find characters who, because of their profession or their personal circumstances, are injured or threatened by the change which makes their world different from the reader's, then you can make the change more meaningful. The reader, in identifying with such characters, will *feel* the effects of the change which has been made rather than simply observing them. If you can then devise for your characters a strategy by which they can recover from their injury, cancel out the threat, or adapt to the situation, that may well provide the ideal plot for your story. Even the most fundamental ideas of sf never get used up, because you can always hunt for a new and better plot to show them off.

This is one of the things which I could not appreciate, and did not try hard enough to do, when I turned out dozens of unsaleable stories in the early part of my career. I thought that ideas were interesting enough on their own, and only had to be revealed in order to interest the reader. For this reason, most of my early stories were entirely devoid of human interest. Nowadays, whenever an idea occurs to me I try to look at it in terms of this perspective.

For instance, I have written a lot of stories about the potential of biotechnology – the possible applications of genetic engineering. This is a field which previous sf has hardly touched, so it is fertile ground for the production of new ideas, but those new ideas still have to be put into plots. In my story "Sexual Chemistry" I posed the question of whether genetic engineers might be able to compensate for the failures of nature by inventing aphrodisiacs that would actually work. I managed to come up with three different kinds of possible aphrodisiacs. In order to work this into a plot I chose as a central character a person whose extreme ugliness gave him a very powerful personal motive for trying to augment his powers of seduction, and then I arranged things so that although his discoveries change the world at large (much more radically than he intends or expects) his own personal problems just get worse, until in the end he manages to solve them more by adjusting his attitude of mind than by means of biotechnological trickery. Though the story is a sarcastic comedy rather than a poignant drama it works on the same principle as Bob Shaw's "Light of Other Days": the idea is made to function within a story by showing its effect on a painful human predicament.

Just as ideas can be unoriginal, so can ways of building them into stories. There are certain clichés which tend to recur frequently. Consider, for instance, the plot in which a man tries to convince a psychiatrist that he is *not* crazy and that people really *are* being replaced by duplicates who are aliens in disguise. Only a naïve reader is going to be surprised by the climactic revelation that the psychiatrist (or the patient) is an alien in disguise, because that kind of inversion of expectation is far too common a trick. In fairness, though, it ought to be pointed out that there is some sf which is directed at audiences which consist very largely of naïve readers; it is therefore not surprising to find that TV sf and sf for children can often trade successfully in ideas and plots which would be considered worn out by the true *aficionado*. Nobody, however, can nowadays get away with the common Victorian stand-by of having your central character wake up to find that whatever has happened to him has only been a dream.

Although the ideas in sf are never completely exhausted – and new developments in real science, like microprocessors and genetic engineering, continually generate new ones – it is nevertheless true that sf writing has changed very dramatically over the years. The fact that many stories have been written about journeys to the moon does not mean that no more can be written, and even the fact that real journeys to the moon have now been made does not mean that there can be no more sf stories involving them. What it *does* mean is that new stories about journeys to the moon must be more sophisticated than their predecessors, and must accept much more demanding standards of plausibility. The kind of rocket which featured in George Pal's film *Destination: Moon* is just as outdated now as the space gun in Jules Verne's *From the Earth to the Moon,* and modern sf writers who want to write near-future stories about space exploration must be prepared to do some research in order to do the job properly.

All kinds of notions which seemed superficially plausible in the 1930s would seem ludicrous today, not only because of progress in real science and technology, but also because the combined imagination of science fiction writers has gradually brought about a sophistication of readers' expectations. We have not yet encountered any real alien beings, but half a century of speculation has served to make the Martians of yesteryear seem all-too-obviously absurd.

Nowadays, sf writers are called upon to be both careful

16

and inventive when they design their aliens. It is normally expected that aliens should make some kind of biological sense, in terms of their anatomy and their ecology. Few people noticed or cared when Edgar Rice Burroughs described a Mars which had lots of nasty predators but no herds of herbivores on which they could prey when not busy threatening the hero and heroine; nor did they worry unduly about the fact that Martian women seemed anatomically very similar to human women despite being egg-layers. Nowadays, a great many readers would feel that their intelligence was being insulted by a writer who unthinkingly committed such follies.

Some ideas which are essentially silly *are* still sanctioned, on the grounds that they are inherently interesting, but even these may alienate some readers if they are presented as if they were seriously-intended. An example of a silly idea which is still sometimes used is the reduction of people to microscopic size. Such stories tend to avoid confronting the thorny question of whether the miniaturized people retain the same mass or not – it is difficult in either case to see how their organs can continue to function, having been either stripped of most of their substance or crushed to an extraordinary density. Such stories survive because the idea gives rise to some fascinating and amusing situations, as displayed in such films as *Fantastic Voyage* and *Inner Space*, but you would have difficulty selling one to a sf magazine like *Analog* unless you were very clever indeed in providing an excuse for the apparent impossibilities.

The nature of sf requires would-be writers to be inventive – which means that they not only have to devise new ways to change the world, but have to convince the reader that what they have done *makes sense.* Then they have to find a story set in their changed world which is an interesting one to tell; ideally, they must find *the* most interesting one to tell. This isn't easy, but when it is done well it provides both its writers and its readers with a special kind of satisfaction, which is well worth striving for.

Chapter Three

The Art of Extrapolation

The word "extrapolation" comes from mathematics, where it refers to the continuation of a line or curve beyond the part which has been mapped out from known information. With reference to the real world we often talk about extrapolating trends, as when we try to estimate the likely future growth of world population by extrapolating the curve which describes population growth during the last fifty or a hundred years. The use of the word has broadened so that any attempt to calculate what is presently unknown by drawing a series of inferences from what *is* known can be called extrapolation.

Sf writers engaged in manufacturing changed worlds are thus engaged in extrapolation. This is most obvious when they are writing about the near future, because in deciding what the near future will be like writers inevitably draw upon their knowledge of present-day trends. It is virtually taken for granted by contemporary writers that the near future will see further increases in world population, increased pollution of the environment, and a great profusion of increasingly clever computers.

It is not only in writing about the future, though, that the writer extrapolates. An alternative history must be extrapolated forward from the point in time when the historical break with our world occurs. This is usually easier, because all those things which would not be affected by the crucial incident can be left to happen exactly as they did in our world.

Because extrapolation of these kinds can be taxing, some sf writers avoid near futures and alternative histories. You can dodge most of the problems of extrapolative reasoning simply by setting your story on another planet, where you can set up situations just as you like. Another common strategy is to write about earthly futures which are disconnected from ours and need not be described by extrapolating present-day trends. It is not too difficult to disconnect futures from the present – a convenient nuclear war, followed by the rebuilding of society from scratch, will do the job nicely.

Writing these kinds of stories does not entirely avoid the problems of extrapolation. In fact, if you take the job of creating a world seriously, and commit yourself to designing an alien biology and an alien society, you may end up doing a great deal of extrapolation. Writers very rarely bother to construct an entire evolutionary history for their imaginary worlds, or an extensive history for their alien societies, but they usually find it necessary to have some vague idea of how the situation which features in their novel came about, and how it might develop in the future. The former is necessary to make the background convincing, the latter is useful in constructing plots where the characters can play for high stakes, with the fate of the world hanging in the balance.

If you want to use an alien world more than once, as many writers tend to do, then the problems of extrapolating its history must be faced. Even if you only want to use it once, an alien society will probably require some kind of history if you are to produce a plot which is interesting and sensible, and that history will have to be determined by "backward extrapolation" from the present which you have designed. If the exotic life-forms which inhabit the planet are to be anything more than fancy decorations, then you may also have to say something in your story about the evolutionary history of the world, which must again be worked out by backward extrapolation. If your planet is to be part of a community of planets – perhaps a galaxy-wide community – then the history of that community too may need extrapolating, insofar as it is going to be relevant to your plot. You need not go into great detail in any of these matters, but you should be prepared to think about them.

This is not necessarily bad news. If you have created an alien world, then you may well be able to take a keen interest in this business of elaborating its history, the evolution of its ecosphere, and its future prospects. After all, the alien planets you invent are *your* worlds and yours alone, and this extrapolation of your inventions is an exercise of your creativity. If you do the job well then you will be able to get a much greater sense of achievement out of it than you could from the work of trying to figure out how our real present is likely to turn into a possible future. It is often intriguing for a reader to watch a writer doing this work of extrapolation in volume after volume of a series featuring an invented world. Frank Herbert's Dune and Marion Zimmer Bradley's Darkover are two of the most extensively-extrapolated imaginary worlds in sf, and many readers have been fascinated by each new episode in the unfolding histories of those worlds.

There is no "correct method" of extrapolation. The people who are interested in the day-to-day business of extrapolation in the real world – weather forecasters, economists, and demographers – are all too well aware of the unreliability of trends. Indeed, the main reason why economic forecasters are interested in trends is so that they can advise the government to take precautionary action when the trends seem to be heading in an undesirable direction. Most of the trends in the human world are things which could be brought under control and turned around, if we cared enough. Sf stories about overpopulated futures are very often stories of the measures which future societies are taking in order to curb further increases in population.

Would-be sf writers should not be tempted to think of their work as an attempt to discover the real shape of the world's future, because that is an impossible project best left to astrologers and other assorted charlatans. But the sf writer must nevertheless take seriously the problem of building plausible connections between the real past and the hypothetical future. You have the job of persuading the reader that the future displayed in your story is a possible outcome of the present. If you are to be reckoned a good writer, then you must be as persuasive as can be – you hit the jackpot when you persuade readers to accept that what you have shown them is well-nigh inevitable, although they never realised it until you pointed it out.

It is probably easier to hit this jackpot when you are

dealing with a world which you have made up yourself, because the reader only knows what you care to reveal, when you care to reveal it, and you have the chance to do a lot of hard thinking about the history and ecology of your world before you first put pen to paper. You have the chance to ask all the necessary questions about the past history of the situation you want to describe, and about the possible ways that it might develop.

When I started out as a science fiction writer I was severely handicapped by being both unable and unwilling to do this work of extrapolation properly. One can perhaps forgive this in the nine-year-old who blithely populated the moon with little men and dinosaurs, unaware of any incongruity in the image, but when I look back at some of my published books I now regret what was nothing more than laziness.

For example, I wrote a series of six novels (beginning with *Halcyon Drift*) which is set some centuries hence in a rapidly-growing galactic community. The hero of the series is infected by a kind of parasite which takes up residence in his brain and generates a mind of its own, with which he holds sharp and sometimes witty dialogues. As a literary device this was very useful; it provided me with some interesting conflicts, a resource which I could use to extricate said hero from awkward situations which he could not have handled on his own, and an easy way to generate yards and yards of padding. The expanding galactic community provided me with an abundance of settings into which he was forced to go in order to help sort out various kinds of problems.

I still think there are some good things about this series, and that some of the exotic life-systems which it features were fairly cleverly extrapolated from my knowledge of biology. By the time I reached the sixth book, though, I was beginning to worry about the background and about the parasite. It was only then that I began to ask myself lots of questions which I really ought to have asked myself before beginning volume one. I had been very slapdash in setting up the galactic community, blithely crediting its legal apparatus to a world called New Rome and its scientific progress to the "library world" of New Alexandria. In fact, it was just a patchwork of bits of our world, writ larger – and most of our world had simply been left out. There were lots of Anglo-American characters, but no real sign of any Japanese or Russian or Africans. There were companies involved in entrepreneurial activities on a galactic scale, but no other visible economic entities.

By volume six I was beginning to ask myself what had happened to all the things that were left out, but it was too late to put them in. I was beginning to wonder how the galactic community had taken up the peculiar form which it had, but I couldn't really figure out a convincing story to account for it. I also began asking myself questions about the parasite which had been chatting away so volubly to the hero. Where had it evolved? What was its natural habitat? What was its history before it conveniently got into my hero? What was it actually made of? If such things existed, why weren't they everywhere in the galaxy? Would everybody want one if they knew they could have one, and could they avoid acquiring one if they didn't? I tried to put in some answers, but it was obvious that they were afterthoughts.

One can, of course, get away with things like that. The majority of galactic communities in sf aren't very much more convincing than mine, and your average sciencefictional mind-parasite is a pretty implausible fellow. I sold the books, they were reasonably successful, and I got far more complaints about the hero's churlish temperament than the matters which had begun to worry me. But the books would have been better by far had I actually done the work of building a more plausible galactic community and extrapolating that fundamental idea. Not only would they have been more plausible; the work of extrapolation would have led me to investigate some avenues of speculation which were interesting in themselves and would have thrown up some intriguing ideas on which plots could be based.

I cannot offer a simple recipe for doing this kind of work, but I do urge you to try to confront such questions before you write your stories. In a way, it doesn't really matter what answers you come up with in reply to the questions – what matters is that you *do* ask the relevant questions. Things you make up on the spur of the moment, carelessly, may be things you can get away with, but they will never be the best things you could have done. The way to write *good* science fiction is to do the best you can to extrapolate your ideas backwards and forwards before you begin to write your stories. If you do the work which is necessary to make the world of your story the kind of world which can contain the things you want to put in it, and the work which will tell you how that world would develop, once those things *are* in it, then you will produce much better stories.

So far, what I have said has been a plea for realism in extrapolation – I have been concerned mainly with plausibility. But plausibility is not the only thing to be considered in making up sf stories. The *art* of extrapolation, as displayed in sf, can be quite different from the *business* of extrapolation used by economic forecasters, because the sf writer's quest is not for the most *likely*, but for the most *interesting* future.

The likeliest futures will not necessarily be exciting ones. Indeed, the near future sf which seems most realistic tends to be a rather grim place, because it tends to be constructed out of all our keenest anxieties. There have been lots of excellent stories set in that world, but the mere fact that we think it likely ensures that it is a familiar image. Careful and sensible extrapolation can easily result in stories which readers will find dull. The artistry of extrapolation, therefore, is often to be seen in the clever connnections which are drawn between our world and a very unusual future, which serve to make that future plausible in spite of its unusualness. Here the extrapolated chain of argument is an excuse rather than a line of logical reasoning.

Futures may be interesting because they are exciting, pregnant with the possibility of a multitude of extravagant adventures, or they may be interesting because they are very frightening, showing us the worst possible things which could happen to the world which we hold in trust for our children and our children's children. Extrapolation in sf, therefore, may quite legitimately want to go beyond the plausible into realms where the imagination can run wild. Wildness of imagination is all the more enjoyable, though, if it does keep some intelligible connection with reality.

There is an effective kind of story-telling which does not try to extrapolate all the trends visible in the real world, but concentrates instead on one particular trend in isolation. Classics of sf like Frederik Pohl and Cyril M. Kornbluth's

The Space Merchants or John Brunner's *Stand on Zanzibar* work by this kind of strategy. The former isolates the techniques of advertising, the latter the effects of overpopulation; both extend the effects of their items of concern so that they become the sole overriding factor determining how life in their imaginary futures is lived. Blowing things up out of all proportion in this manner is a standard method in satire, and sf stories like these often take on a satirical edge, but they need not go so far as to become grotesque.

We can also see this same concentration on a single topic of concern in some fine stories where the work of extrapolation has been done backwards. It is often the case that in creating a purely imaginary world an author wants to isolate some single point of crucial difference between that world and our own. Thus, Theodore Sturgeon in *Venus Plus X* and Ursula le Guin in *The Left Hand of Darkness* both devise a sciencefictional logic which makes it possible to have a world in which male and female are not differentiated as they are in our world – where the people are hermaphrodites of some kind.

The work of extrapolation in these examples consisted of asking how such a thing might be biologically possible, then asking what kind of history and what kind of future prospects the worlds which could contain such possibilities might have. Sturgeon and le Guin then set their plots in motion by introducing into their imaginary worlds an observer from a world where the sexes *are* differentiated in the way familiar to us. They allow their observers to learn about the new world, to attempt to enter into its way of life, and finally to pass some sort of judgment on the relative merits of the two ways of being. Both of these examples are earnest and careful experiments in thought, but many less intense stories are doing the same kind of thing in a lighter vein.

The artistry of extrapolation is much the same whether the sf writer wants to extrapolate forwards, by looking at the present situation and trying to find interesting possibilities which might emerge from it, or backwards, by imagining an interesting possibility and then trying to figure out a way in which it could have come about. In each case it is a matter of trying to build a chain of cause-and-effect which makes some sort of sense. You have to persuade the reader to allow, for the sake of the story, that things really could be the way you say they are, and really would go on the way you say they are going to. The reader always *wants* to be persuaded, but will feel justifiably let down if you fail to provide an argument with some genuine persuasive power. Naïve readers may be very easily persuaded, and this allows a certain latitude for carelessness or ineptitude; but the more work you put into the artistry of extrapolation, the more readers you will be able to reach, and the more admirable a writer you will be.

A demanding reader may also feel let down if, at the end of a sf story, confrontation with the imaginary world has not in some way affected his attitude to the real world. For this reason, the connections which you make between your futures and the real present, or between the past and present of your inaginary worlds, should be ones which are ingenious as well as plausible. Even in stories which – unlike *The Space Merchants* or *The Left Hand of Darkness* – can be regarded as "pure entertainment" or "pure escapism" what happens, if it is to be really enjoyable, ought to have some kind of relationship with the real world. Nonsense is fun because of its contrast with sense, and fantastic dream-worlds are exciting because of the ways in which they defy and compensate for the particular deficiencies and frustrations of reality. The cleverer you are at building the connections which link the elements of your story to the real world of your readers, the more you will deserve – and obtain – the applause of those readers.

Chapter Four

Describing a Different World

All writers have to cope with the problem of telling the readers what they need to know about the place where the story is set, and the difficulties which they face depend largely on the strangeness of their setting.

When writers who set their stories in contemporary London or New York say that this is where the action can take place they can then assume that the vast majority of their readers will already know a great deal about those settings – TV and film have made those places familiar to us even if personal acquaintance has not. But a writer who wishes to set a novel in some remote period of Chinese history knows that most of the readers who pick up the book will have very little idea of what to expect, and must confront the thorny question of what to say, at what point in the narrative, and in what way, about what the houses look like, what the people wear, and what sort of things the characters do in the normal course of their affairs.

Sf writers are apparently in the worst position of all, because their stories are often set in wholly imaginary worlds about which the reader knows nothing until he is told. Even if I were to begin reading a historical novel about China I would have some resources on which to draw – I know what a Chinaman looks like, and I have some vague idea of the level of technological development which I might find. I may not have much of an idea about when the Great Wall of China was built, or when Genghis Khan lived, or when Marco Polo visited the Far East, but if it so happens that references to these matters crop up in the story, I have something graspable which will allow me to be more easily enlightened. But when I start a science fiction novel set on a planet which orbits a distant star I know nothing at all about its biology, its inhabitants or its technology. Everything that I need to know about these things the writer will have to tell me, but it may make the story difficult and dull to read if the writer puts in huge slabs of explanatory prose – a practice sometimes known as "info-dumping".

This situation is not as problematic as it seems. In some ways it can be an advantage to a writer to be able to work with an entirely imaginary world. We can see why when we think about the usefulness of imaginary worlds in the stories which parents tell small children.

From the point of view of the young child the real world is a very complicated place, almost totally unknown, and the child's experience of it is very different from the adult's. It is very difficult for the parent to tell the child stories about the real world, because many things which the parent takes for granted would puzzle the child. When talking about the real world, or a fictional world supposed to be real, parent and child do not, and cannot, "speak the same language". Fairyland is much more convenient, because the parent and the child are on common ground. All that the child knows about Fairyland is what the story says about it, and that is all the parent knows, too, because it is all there is to know. Fairyland can be made as simple as it needs to be, stocked with characters who can be described in the most elementary terms: beautiful or ugly, brave or cowardly, young or old, king or peasant, good or evil. There is a sense in which parent and child communicate much more easily when they are talking about fairyland than when they are talking about the real world, which they see in very different terms.

This is one reason why children tend to like fantastic fiction, and why teenagers may find sf easier to relate to than complicated fictions about the real world. The vast majority of people prefer reading stories set in places with which they are not familiar. The tip sheets which publishers of romances often give out to writers to explain the rigid formulas which such stories tend to follow often insist that the ritualistic story of boy-meets-girl/they-have-problems/they-get-together should be set in some exotic location. Whole genres of fiction are defined by their exotic locations: historical novels, westerns, war stories. Even stories which are notionally set in the contemporary world are often displaced to social settings very different from those of the majority of readers: English detective stories often used to be set at country house-parties; the school stories read by generations of day school boys were typically set in public schools; the best-selling dramas enjoyed by the super-poor usually deal with the sins and passions of the super-rich. It is hardly surprising that reading is often described as a kind of "escapism".

For this reason, filling in background detail is a problem much commoner in writing fiction than it may seem, and it is often solved by the deceptively simple strategy of leaving things out.

Readers can orientate themselves within the world of a story with surprising ease. This is partly because they carry forward an understanding from other stories of a similar type – thus, for instance, the writer of westerns can rely upon the fact that the habitual reader already knows a great deal about the kind of setting which his story will have (a setting which, of course, bears very little resemblance to any historical reality). Although the sf reader cannot rely on the fictional worlds which he enters being as similar as the overlapping imaginary worlds of western fiction, he does have expectations gathered under such rough headings as "near futures", "post-holocaust scenarios", "alien planets", etc.

Because of this, scene-setting can often be done with much more economy of effort than you might think. Try re-reading a story which you have enjoyed with an analytical eye, to see exactly how much information is given; you will find that it is surprisingly little, and will then realise how clever and skillful the average reader is in building a notion of what the world of a story is like from so very few clues.

Descriptive prose *can* be like pre-Raphaelite painting, attempting to specify the colour, position and texture of every object which a hypothetical observer would see, but it is usually far more like drawing a cartoon, where a few well-chosen lines reproduce the key features of a face and a setting. The cleverest description is the one which persuades the reader, by a kind of confidence trick, that you have laid out a great deal of information when in fact you have given only the barest essentials. This is necessary in short stories, where there simply is not space for elaborate description.

A common technique used in describing exotic locations is to assume the viewpoint of someone already at home in that environment, who simply refers to things briefly and matter-of-factly. That way, your reader can be informed about the sort of things which are around without any kind of elaboration. Even when the viewpoint is not tied to a particular person this kind of laconic reference is possible. Consider, for instance, the first line of George Orwell's *Nineteen Eighty-Four*: "It was a bright cold day in April and the clocks were striking thirteen." This judicious mixture of the ordinary and the unexpected tells us immediately that we are in a strange world, and makes the reader alert to what might be coming next. Orwell then moves swiftly to a description of a face on a poster, above the legend: BIG BROTHER IS WATCHING YOU. This relatively bald description is a vital piece of information masquerading as a trivial detail, for the fact that Big Brother is everywhere and watching is the central fact of Orwell's imaginary world. Already, at the end of page one, we have a fair idea where and when we are, and what kind of thing we must look out for in the pages to come.

Writers and readers have long grown used to this style of presentation; it is as if there exists a conspiracy or contract whereby the reader simply does not expect to be told in great detail exactly what is happening or where. In reading, most of the labour of imagining what places and people look like is accepted by the reader and in fact is never done. When people watch films or TV dramatisations of books which they have read they are very often quite startled by the visual appearances which the film-maker has been forced by his medium to fill in. They often say "I thought of the character as a different sort of person," or "That wasn't the way I imagined the room/city/forest," but this is sometimes slightly hypocritical, because it is perfectly possible to read printed texts without making any real attempt to visualise the people, places and events which are described there.

Writers still have to do some clever work to fulfil their side of the tacit bargain. The essential information must still be set down, one way or another. A writer certainly must not leave the reader lacking any point of information about what things look like, or what objects are to hand, which is actually going to be significant in the plot. In addition, the writer must provide enough clues for readers to feel that they have an adequate grasp of the kind of environment in which the story is taking place.

This is made easier for writers using stereotyped settings, real or imaginary, because the writers can simply signal the relevant stereotype and plug in to what the reader already knows. Much of the labour of description can easily be taken up by mentioning the respects in which the environment of the story *differs* from the stereotype which the reader is already assumed to know – a surprising amount of description consists of informing the reader of what things are not.

What sf readers already know when they begin a new story is less than the reader of westerns or war stories already knows, but they nevertheless do carry forward from their previous reading an approximate understanding of what the story is likely to contain, and have in mind a number of stereotypes which the writer can use, negatively – by saying what his milieu is not like – if not positively. The habitual sf reader already has a vague knowledge of kinds of spaceships or galactic communities which can be brought into play fairly readily with a single key reference, and the habitual sf reader will quickly pick up on the little clue you use to signal that this one is an alternative history story. In characterising an alien planet the writer can usually liken it to some exemplars which the reader already has in his vocabulary – the moon, Mars, and most especially Earth – and it is also possible to specify quickly and easily those significant respects in which the imaginary world is *not* like Earth.

Readers do have to learn to pick up and use these clues, but they are surprisingly adept at learning the ropes, so that they can draw the inferences which help them to locate a story relative to the catalogue of possible future-types or imaginary world-types. You do not need to start from scratch when you set out to tell your readers what kind of setting they are using; you can and should exploit to the full the context of expectation which most readers already have. It is usually not a good idea to start your story with a long info-dump sequence giving a full history or essay on the biology of your imaginary world. Information is best intruded by degrees into a story which is already moving along, hopefully without slowing down its pace too much. If you *do* need a substantial info-dump, save it for a pause in the action, and if you follow the customary practice of having one character explain all the necessary things in conversation with another, try to make certain that the person to whom things are being explained really is in need of enlightenment, and try to lighten the conversation with the odd intelligent question or witticism.

Naïve readers can, of course, be utterly bewildered by the moves which a writer makes, and may not be able to infer as much as they are supposed to. It does take practice to learn the conventions of a genre, and sf is one which makes unusually heavy demands on the acumen of its readers. Most readers are tolerant about this, and are often prepared to be bewildered by what they read. There are, however, some people who have developed a kind of imaginative allergy to sf because they simply could not get the hang of the texts which they tried to read, and became annoyed. It is partly because of the relative difficulty of "learning to read sf" that the genre took time to catch on and expand its market. It is not surprising that John Wyndham, who specialised in catastrophe stories which begin in the familiar world, was the first British writer to reach a wider readership in the 1950s, when sf was still fairly esoteric. Nor is it surprising that TV programmes like *Star Trek* have been enormously successful in recruiting new sf fans, even though they cannot possibly reproduce on the screen the kinds of things which happen in most sf stories; however silly their visual representations are, they provide an easy way for people to get the hang of finding their way around the imaginary universe of a sf story.

Most beginning writers do not realise how little they have to specify in their descriptions, and it is very common to find stories by novice writers which are interrupted by long descriptive passages. Sometimes the descriptions are interesting, but over-elaborate description is a terrible handicap to the pace of a story. Your reader will usually thank you for

31

getting to the heart of the action as quickly as possible, and if you fail to maintain momentum, you may lose your reader altogether.

When I first started out I wrote a great many "stories" which contained very little *but* description of exotic places. Even when I had learned that the only way to make such descriptions acceptable as elements of a story was to make them the setting of violent and exciting adventures, I still produced stories which were like stage plays in which men in funny costumes fought one another in front of garish backcloths. There are a lot of such stories about, and they can be fun to read, but they are usually rather weak.

My earliest novels, especially *Cradle of the Sun* and *To Challenge Chaos*, provide unfortunate examples of over-abundant and not very useful description. They follow the most elementary formula of plot construction. *Cradle of the Sun* (the novel I wrote in ten days when I was nineteen) begins by giving a group of characters a reason for undertaking a journey; the middle of the book consists simply of a series of descriptions of different places through which they pass, in each case being threatened by some kind of hostile action – usually involving a monster – which they have to defeat; at the end, the sole survivor succeeds (after a fashion) in doing what he set out to do. *To Challenge Chaos* takes the same formula to bizarre lengths. In these works the painstaking description of exotic places merely compensates for the absence of any real plot, and the descriptions themselves are simply accounts of strange entities unsupported by any kind of biological logic. Nowadays, when I describe strange and exotic settings, I want them to make some sort of biological sense, and I also want them to have some sort of integral part in the scheme of my story.

The story told in my recent series of novels *Journey to the Centre* is an action-packed adventure in exotic surroundings with no more pretensions to profundity than *Cradle of the Sun* had, but its use of strange settings is very much better. The regions which the characters visit are described much more economically, and the plot revolves around their attempts to explore and explain what they find. It is bad practice to use exotic environments simply to provide arbitrary backcloths for the action; even action-adventure stories benefit enormously if the settings form some kind of coherent whole, and if their oddities are made significant within the plot.

I must confess, though, that I remain an unrepentant wholesale info-dumper. I do like to put in explanations of the biology of the environments through which my characters move, and of other elements in my story. I have often found myself in conflict with editors who think that I do this far too much; my short stories are often rejected because of the "lectures" in them, and editors are always trying to hype up the pace of my novels by cutting the background information. I honestly believe that many sf readers actually appreciate a bit of background information now and again, and will forgive the occasional interruption of the action. Even in those of my novels which I remember with pride, therefore, the reader is apt to stumble across long, deep conversations or chunks excerpted from imaginary reference books.

Even if you side with the editors and not with me on this matter of info-dumping, you will still have to get your own information in somehow. You may be able to signal to your readers easily and economically what sort of world they are in, but you must nevertheless take care to tell them every specific thing that they will need to know about it. You must tell them everything which is relevant to your story, even if you tell them no more. If it does not matter in any way what people are wearing, then you may simply not bother to mention it, or just make incidental reference to shirts and trousers, but if the progress of the story is going to depend on the particular features of the space-suit that your hero is wearing, then you have to fill in those details *before* you get to the point in the story where they become vital.

Playwrights are often advised that they should not clutter up the stage set with items which are not going to be used, but that everything which the characters will need should not only be there but be *seen to be there*. If a character is going to take a gun out of a drawer in Act Three it is necessary to find some way of letting the audience know that it is there in Act One; that way they get a sense of events flowing naturally rather than things developing arbitrarily. Story-writers must take care to do the same.

Everything which is vital to your story, whether it be an instrument which figures in the action or a detail which will enable the hero to solve a puzzle, must be put in as early as possible, and as unobtrusively as possible. A surprise twist in a plot will only delight readers if they have been given the information required to set it up.

This is one reason why writers usually need to write at least two drafts of a story. I always try to work out a story pretty thoroughly in advance, but it usually happens that the flow of development carries it in an unexpected direction, or that I get to a certain place and realise that I have made inadequate provision for getting my character to the next relevant point in the plot. If he now needs a pen-knife or a calculator which I unfortunately failed to place in his pocket when he set out, then I have to go back to the point where he set out and write in the relevant item.

In addition to providing the information about the setting which will figure importantly in the story, a certain amount of descriptive work does have to be done in the interests of "local colour". You do have to give readers a sense of place and a sense of character. Arbitrary details add materially to the sense of strangeness which sf writers often want to cultivate, and the intrusion of oddities for the sake of reminding the readers that they are in a strange world is useful. It can also be a pleasant exercise of pure creative energy. In addition, some incidental detail will inevitably be necessary to provide a background into which essential information can fade – you do not want to advertise too blatantly *which* bits of information are going to be relevant if you are to maintain suspense. This is especially important if your plot is going to present your characters with a puzzle to be solved. Surprising your reader is usually a matter of camouflaging the vital bit of information so that he will not bring it to mind even though he will remember, when you explain how vital it is, that he has been shown it.

Generally speaking, you should integrate description and action as cleverly and as seamlessly as you can. If you want to specify the presence of an object, mention someone using it rather than simply observing that it is lying on a table. Describe places from the viewpoint of someone approaching or moving through them. This maintains the flow of the story, maintaining your reader's interest in it. You do not need, however, to take this advice to extremes. Sometimes, it will be necessary for your characters to pause, and it is often convenient for them to express wonder at the sights which confront them.

When your characters arrive for the first time in a new place – which will in many sf stories be a place which no one has ever seen or imagined before – you will certainly want to describe the scene, and comment on the shock which it causes. Static description is in those circumstances unavoidable, and you must do your best to provide a description which will do justice to the amazing place you have created. Bear in mind while you plan your story that too much static description can be a dead weight slowing it down, even if you are describing the most wonderful places ever imagined, but do make room for the occasional expression of the sheer fantasticality of the world you have invented.

At such moments of awesome revelation, which are a key element in very many sf and fantasy stories, you *can* get away with torrents of adjectives and long passages offering detailed accounts of astonishing objects. Despite what conventional style-guides say about the horrors of adjective-laden "purple prose" it is unreasonable to ask of would-be sf writers that they should always avoid the temptation to indulge themselves. There is simply too much scope in sf for going over the top, and one of the reasons for reading and writing sf is to savour those dislocations of perspective which occur when characters and readers move together from a narrow and tawdry world into a vaster and more gorgeous one. Ration such moments, lest they test the patience of the reader whose main interest is finding out what happened next, but when the moment comes, you are quite entitled to let yourself go.

Chapter Five
Worldbuilding

Designing your own world can be a fascinating and enjoyable exercise, and is one which many sf writers approach with enthusiasm. When my schoolfriend and I planned the novel which we wrote in our early teens the first thing we did was draw a map of the island continent on an alien world where most of the action was to take place. Then we filled in all the details of mountains, swamps and so on, decided where the spaceship was going to land, and mapped out the explorations which our characters would undertake. It was fun – in fact, this sort of thing can be much more fun than writing the story, and it is probable that many projects never get further than this pre-planning stage.

Mapmaking is, of course, the most elementary exercise in world design. What my schoolfriend and I did, more-or-less unthinkingly, was to assume that conditions on our imaginary world would be much the same as they are on Earth, save for a few purely cosmetic alterations: a touch more oxygen in the atmosphere, a much higher ratio of sea to land and (for melodramatic purposes) giant insects. The fact that there is a connection between the amount of oxygen in a planetary atmosphere and the photosynthetic activity of plants was quite unknown to us, so we never bothered to specify where one would find the extra biomass that might be responsible for the excess oxygen – but a tiny slip like that would have been no barrier to publication.

The great majority of worlds featured in sf stories have been manufactured in this very simple fashion: they are mostly Earth-clones with a dash of colour. The same is true of the Secondary Worlds of fantasy, which tend to be alternative Earths in a very narrow sense. There are, however, a minority of imaginary worlds in sf which have been designed in a much more comprehensive fashion, with physical conditions and life-systems very different from those of Earth.

From the point of view of the expert worldbuilder, Earth-clones are mere finger-exercises. Those sf writers who have a sound knowledge of the relevant sciences delight in trying to figure out what conditions might really be like on the surfaces of worlds which are physically very different from Earth, and they are very rigorous in extrapolating a few premises into a landscape with figures. It is a game which has attracted painters, too – painting convincing and hopefully accurate landscapes set on other worlds (usually the other worlds in the solar system as defined by astronomical discovery) has long been a preoccupation of artists like Chesley Bonestell and David Hardy.

The first sf writer to make a name for himself by the exercise of his worldbuilding ingenuity was Hal Clement. His most famous novel, *Mission of Gravity*, is set on a world called Mesklin which is much larger than Earth, but which rotates on its axis very quickly. This has the effect that the pull of gravity exerts a much greater force than we are used to at the poles, but rather less at the equator (because of the compensating effect of centrifugal force).

The calculation of physical conditions like gravity and atmospheric conditions is only the first part of the world-builder's task, because these must then be taken to be the fundamental forces of natural selection which determine what kind of life-forms could have evolved on the imaginary world. In *Mission of Gravity* Clement concludes that the gravitational conditions on Mesklin would favour many-legged ground-hugging creatures built rather like millipedes, and an intelligent individual of this kind is one of the heroes of his story.

Exotic worldbuilding is something which is very rarely done well in sf. In the days of pulp sf writers would blithely set stories on Mercury or Jupiter without trying to take into account anything which was known about those planets – even such elementary matters as gravity, temperature and atmosphere. A writer who did that today would seem rather stupid, and this is one reason why sf writers deserted the solar system in droves in the 1940s and 1950s, so that they could make their Earth-clone planets safe from the ravages of the astronomical data which tell us that conditions on the surfaces of our neighbouring planets are very different indeed from those on our own fair homeworld.

Writers who lack Clement's expertise but who want to do a respectable job of describing a peculiar alien world will usually seek expert help, as Brian Aldiss did in calculating the eccentric orbit and designing the biology of Helliconia. There is scope for more serious collaboration, as was seen when Harlan Ellison instigated the teaming up of a number of writers to determine the physics, biology and history of an imaginary world which then became the setting for ten stories written by them – a description of the project is included with the stories in the anthology *Medea: Harlan's World* edited by Ellison. "Shared world" anthologies have since become more common, but very few of them involve determined exercises in exotic worldbuilding.

It is not simply laziness or incompetence, though, which leads most sf writers to prefer Earth-clones as settings for their stories. Human characters can only function in a truly alien environment with great difficulty. Different gravity will affect their every movement, and a different atmosphere will make it necessary for them to walk around in something like a spacesuit. This not only narrows the possible range of plots, but it puts an extraordinarily heavy burden on the writer's ability to explain what is going on and the reader's capacity for understanding his explanations – exotic world-builders have to do a *lot* of info-dumping.

For this reason there are many readers who are quite willing to concede that a book like *Mission of Gravity* is an imaginative *tour de force* but will add that it was nevertheless rather hard to read. The situation is not helped by the narrowing of plot-opportunities open to the writer. Plots which can adequately display the hard work and ingenuity which the writer has put into the design of his world usually involve a journey across its surface, and though the journey can be made suspenseful by making it a race against time, or a chase, or a battle for survival, there is always the danger that it might deteriorate into an exercise in imaginary tourism. It is easier for a writer to become engrossed in such a project than a reader – we are always more interested in our own holiday snaps than other people's.

The game of designing life-systems to fit very exotic physical conditions is intriguing enough to ensure that sf continually throws up new and more daring examples. Robert Forward's novel *Dragon's Egg* imagines intelligent life evolving on the surface of a neutron star, while Larry Niven's *The Integral Trees* features a life-system which has no planet at all, and such life-systems certainly have a measure of fascination which excuses a bit of stodgy plotting. But Forward and Niven are pastmasters in the art of world-building, and the novice writer ambitious to emulate them has a Herculean task on hand.

There is, however, still considerable scope for cleverness in worldbuilding even if you begin by accepting that your imaginary world must be similar enough to Earth to allow human beings to move and breathe quite comfortably. The same physical conditions can be combined with a wide range of biological conditions.

The life-forms which currently exist on Earth are the result of a particular historical sequence which might have turned out very differently had some relatively trivial change been introduced at a strategic point some time during the last billion years. Such a change might involve a catastrophe – it is at least possible that the evolutionary course of life on Earth has been affected by collisions between Earth and large meteors, and that things would have been different had there been more meteor-strikes, or less, or had the meteors struck at different times. Even if one assumes that there were no events of that kind, the random mutation of genes might easily have thrown up something new, or failed to produce some vital gene. The Earth-clones of sf, therefore, can be populated with a great variety of plausible and rationally defensible life-systems.

This is my favourite kind of sciencefictional speculation, because it is the one where my own expertise happens to lie. I did my first degree in biology, and the aspects of biological science which fascinated me most were evolution and genetics. I find it fascinating to employ these theories to work out coherent and believable "alternative ecospheres" which I can then deploy in my stories. My six volume *Daedalus* series presents a series of such worlds, the central characters visiting each one in turn to find out how human colonies have fared. It was the fundamental assumption of the series that colonising even the most Earthlike of planets would prove difficult because of the delicacy of our own ecological relationships with other Earthly species. I have to admit that although I found the business of designing the worlds fascinating, many readers were unable to share the fascination, some complaining about excessive info-dumping and unsatisfactory plots. (I don't suppose they'd have enjoyed looking at my holiday snaps, either.)

The fact that I regard designing life-systems as my own particular forte has the further effect that I find it difficult to read sf stories where the author has made mistakes in that area, or not thought things through. When the ecology of an alien world seems to me to be incoherent or unconvincing it can spoil my enjoyment of a story, though I can still find some purpose in reading it by looking upon it as a specimen to be dissected. Being well aware that others do not necessarily share this hypercritical outlook I find myself in a dilemma as to what advice I should honestly offer the would-be writer. My conscience urges me to plead with you to try to get it *right*, but realism suggests that I come clean and admit that if you get it a little bit wrong, the majority of readers will not notice, and those who do will probably be willing to forgive you.

I think the most sensible advice that I can offer to would-be worldbuilders is to exploit your own particular strength, wherever it may lie. I could never match someone like Hal Clement in designing physically exotic worlds, and I will never try. On the other hand, I do not think there are many people who can design alternative Earthlike ecospheres as well as I can, so that is where I will continue to invest my most elaborate creative effort. But even if I had no expertise at all in the natural sciences there would still be scope for me to operate as an sf writer. Even if the physical and biological differences between your imaginary world and Earth are purely cosmetic, there remain opportunities for designing weird quasi-human societies. Because the social sciences are less exact than the natural sciences, it is much harder for anyone to tell you that you have made a mistake in designing an exotic society, so this becomes a game that almost anyone can play and win.

In most sf, alien societies are usually assumed to be much like ours. The aliens might look peculiar but they behave in much the same way as characters in any other action-adventure story, and their way of life is clearly based on ours – they have politicians and generals, banks and drinking-dens, sporting events and trials, marriages and funerals. Aliens are very often more barbaric than we are, though they sometimes consider us to be the barbarians, but in the plots of sf stories they tend to fit into stereotyped roles not too different from those allotted to red indians in westerns or Russians in spy stories. This may seem like a sad failure of imagination, but it is understandable when we remember that the only example of a radically different kind of "society" which we have available to us is the ant-hive. Hive-societies, in fact, crop up very frequently as a model for alien societies, from Wells' *The First Men in The Moon* onwards, but for the most part, alien societies have to be based more-or-less loosely on human societies.

As sf has become more sophisticated, though, writers have drawn more and more on the insights of social science, particularly anthropology. Many contemporary writers have equipped themselves to construct more complicated and more convincing alien societies by familiarising themselves with the actual range of human societies, and by taking the trouble to look at the different ways in which human societies are organised. The insights of anthropology are limited – the human societies which are very different from ours are of course preliterate societies, most useful for helping us design technologically primitive aliens – but they have been used to good effect. Ursula le Guin, whose father Alfred Kroeber was one of the great names in anthropology, has drawn upon this resource very cleverly; a good example is her novella *The Word for World is Forest*. Writers have similarly tried to draw upon other areas of human science, including linguistics, in order to help them design more complex and more convincing alien societies; some of the works of C. J. Cherryh, including the recent *Cuckoo's Egg*, provide good examples of how this is done.

When you want to approach the task of building an imaginary world, therefore, you should ask yourself what kind of knowledge you already have – or what kind of research you could most conveniently do – which could provide you with the resources to make your world both intelligently and interestingly different from ours. If you have no such knowledge, and cannot be bothered with research, then you had best put your efforts into the construction of a very exciting plot, because any world you build will only be Earth in fancy dress, and your aliens will only be human actors in lurid make-up. This will not prevent you from writing and selling stories set in the far-flung outposts of the galactic empire, but there will always be some churlish readers (me included) who will grumpily argue that what you are writing is not "real sf".

Worldbuilding is not easy, and the more fundamental the level is at which you make your world different from Earth, the more difficult the task is which you have set yourself. But this kind of work is also a kind of play, and there is a special satisfaction to be derived from success in the game. Writers of mundane fiction may have to do a good deal of research into the particular society or period of time in which their stories are set, but their triumphs can only ever be triumphs of *re*-creation. Sf writers have the opportunity to make worlds of their own, and though they must play by certain rules which the universe lays down for them, they have the chance to come up with something that nobody ever thought of before. It is a rare privilege to be able to contemplate a new world which you have created, and the privilege is all the greater if you are able to declare that it is a *possible* world; a world which *makes sense*.

Chapter Six
Imaginary Hardware

It was the advancing pace of technological change in the real world which first inspired the writing of sf stories. The first sf writers, excited by the new discoveries which were transforming their own lives, rushed to anticipate the adventures which further inventions would make possible. Jules Verne and his contemporaries wrote enthusiastically about submarines, aeroplanes and spaceships, about bigger and better guns and bigger and better bombs. When Röntgen discovered X-rays at the end of the nineteenth century there was an immediate boom in stories about miraculous new rays which would heal or kill, transform or disintegrate. The history of sf is on the one hand a celebration of the power of the machine to increase the scope of human opportunity, and on the other a catalogue of anxieties about the ways in which individuals and whole societies might use the power of technology destructively.

Many champions of sf, in the days when it was commonly derided as an essentially silly form of literature, claimed that sf writers often showed extraordinary powers of foresight in their depictions of future technology. The pioneering pulp magazine *Amazing Stories* carried on its title page the slogan "Extravagant Fiction Today – Cold Fact Tomorrow", recalling with pride that the imaginary submarines and aeroplanes of fiction were quickly supplemented by real ones. *Amazing Stories* and the other sf pulps certainly carried forward the tradition: the sf reader was familiar with mechanical brains long before the first computer was built, with powerful rays long before the first laser, and with robots long before the word was borrowed from sf stories and applied to real machines. The two greatest anticipatory triumphs of sf were, of course, the atom bomb and the moon-rocket; the second triumph was aknowledged when both NASA and the TV networks covering the first lunar landing felt it appropriate that sf writers should be on hand to accept a measure of congratulation.

Actually, the powers of foresight possessed by sf writers have (like the successes of all would-be prophets) been somewhat inflated in retrospect. The anticipations of *20,000 Leagues Under the Sea* seem slightly less marvellous when one discovers that Jules Verne had actually seen a prototype submarine, *Le Plongeur*, on exhibition in Paris some years before writing his novel – it was one of several which had undergone trial submersions. The illustrations for the book, which show men in diving suits resembling the real thing, are a little less impressive when one reads the text description carefully and realises that their use would have been fatal because Verne had overlooked the necessity of pressurising them. On the other hand, it does seem to have been the case that the 20th century scientists who did the actual research in rocketry which eventually put a man on the moon were nearly all inspired to do it by the sf which they read in their youth.

The sf writer who wants to take the design of futuristic technology seriously has to be very clever. The task is not impossible, because advances in scientific theory may convince us that certain kinds of machine are theoretically possible long before engineers solve the practical problems of construction. Thus, sf writer Arthur C. Clarke was able to develop the idea of the communications satellite some years before there were rockets capable of putting such satellites into orbit.

Sf writers often work within this margin between theoretical and practical possibility. Sf writers of the forties, having read up on nuclear fission, could write fairly plausible stories about accidents in nuclear power plants, so that Lester del Rey's "Nerves" (1942) has come to seem disturbingly prophetic in the wake of Three Mile Island and Chernobyl. Sf writers of today who want to write about fusion reactors have a great deal of published research to draw on, and can achieve a considerable degree of realism even though no one in the real world has yet managed to make a fusion reaction produce more energy than was used to start it up.

By the same token, sf writers wishing to design convincing

spaceships can draw upon various resources in terms of theoretical means of propulsion, and in terms of the work done by space scientists preparing for the day when their drawing-board dreams will be put into production. David Langford's book *War in 2080* and the chapters which he contributed to *The Science in Science Fiction* edited by Peter Nicholls provide excellent illustrations of the way that imaginary hardware can be "invented" by extrapolating from scientific theory.

Arthur C. Clarke is an ingenious and prolific designer of hypothetical machinery, and his near future stories of the exploration of the solar system set a remarkable standard of realism. It is not simply that his machines are convincing in isolation, but that he integrates them together into coherent descriptions of everyday life in spaceships and space stations, or in bases on other worlds. These descriptions have an air of authenticity which is very difficult for would-be competitors to duplicate. Mercifully, the beginning writer who wants to set stories in environments of this kind does not have to start from scratch. Hypothetical machines and hypothetical environments quickly become common property, and writers are perfectly entitled to borrow them provided that they do not copy detailed descriptions.

It is important for the would-be sf writer to realise, though, that not all imaginary hardware belongs to the category of possible-but-not-yet-practical machinery. There are "machines" in sf which perform a very different literary function, the archetype of the species being H. G. Wells' time machine.

Wells' Time Traveller does provide us with an account of the "theory" behind his machine, and a sketchy description of what it looks like, but this is mere bluff. What Wells is doing is *pretending* to explain, while really only providing a "jargon of apology". Wells "invented" a time machine not because he thought that it would one day be possible for one to be built in reality, but because it was such a very useful literary device. With one bold stroke of the imagination the entire future of the world suddenly became open to inspection, and the time traveller's task in determining the destiny of the human race became as easy as riding a bicycle. Here, imaginary technology features as a kind of licensed magic, whose job is simply to make the impossible believable.

Usually, when sf writers allow their characters to explain

how spaceships or time machines work, they are entering into another of those tacit conspiracies in which writer and reader join. The author puts on a show of demonstrating that the story *is* dealing in possibilities, by throwing around a few phrases which sound scientific because of the jargon they use; the reader is in consequence prepared to accept the ensuing adventures as credible, taking them as seriously as if they were accounts of mundane events.

It is very difficult to judge how far readers really are taken in by this kind of performance, and to what extent they are aware of the fact that they are only observing a ritual. I was once quite surprised when a reader told me how impressed he was by the passage in my novel *Halcyon Drift* where a new spaceship first takes off. "Of course," he said, "I didn't understand a word of it, but it was very convincing."

It is hardly surprising that the reader in question didn't understand a word of it, because the passage is pure gibberish. The words were chosen because they sounded vaguely like the sort of things and processes which one might find in a spaceship's engine (sorry, its *drive*): there was a thing called a "piledriver" and some stuff called "flux", and it was all fitted together by a "mass-relaxation web", which was controlled by the pilot through a "nerve-net".

I have never thought of passages like this as attempts to cheat or mislead the reader, and I do not expect anyone to be fooled into thinking that I know what I am talking about. But some such effort is necessary to maintain the pretence that the story is taking place in a future world, where all sorts of things incomprehensible to us are so familiar that people take them entirely for granted and refer to them in an off-hand way, as if they expected everyone to understand what they meant.

Given that these made-up pseudotechnical descriptions are nonsense, you might think that they would be very easy to do, but in fact this can be hazardous ground for the unwary. I can only compare the situation to the rules of etiquette which used to govern behaviour in high society in the 18th and 19th centuries. Absurd as it may seem, arbitrary and meaningless jargon terms can date very badly, and some imaginary machines which were once acceptable as devices in sf plots now belong to the category of things which are simply *not done*.

One staple of pulp sf was the translation machine, which enabled travellers from Earth to establish communications with aliens with consummate ease. The absurdity of the notion is parodied quite neatly by Douglas Adams, whose galactic hitch-hikers achieve the same end by inserting "Babel fish" into their ears. It is now taken for granted that instant translation machines are too silly to be sanctioned, and humans contacting aliens have to do things the hard way.

Most of sf's wonderful rays have gone the same way. Back in the 1930s it was perfectly acceptable for scientists to discover Q-rays and Z-rays or (if they were classically educated) *theta*-rays and *zeta*-rays, which could blithely be given credit for doing almost anything, from disintegrating metals to making people immortal. Nowadays, the scientist called upon to explain how his new machine works is simply not allowed to say "Well, it all began when I discovered the secret of the Q-ray . . ." Explanations like that never did make any sense, but they have somehow lost the warrant which let them *pretend* to make sense in times gone by.

Given that much of the machinery in sf is really disguised magic, and that the "explanations" of its working are fake, it is not easy to determine why some fakes pass muster while others don't. As with other matters, it does depend to some extent on the assumed naïvety of the audience – TV and comic book writers take much greater liberties than the editors of the sf magazines would allow. It is as though there were continual negotiations going on between the Vernian hardware extrapolators who are trying to determine what kind of machines might result from the application of contemporary scientific knowledge and the Wellsian adventurers who just want something that will get the characters to the interesting places with no bother, and give them what they need to work the required miracles. The latter are always borrowing from the former, greedily appropriating new devices and discoveries for their own purposes, and it is as if the *quid pro quo* for that wholesale borrowing allows the hardware extrapolators limited powers of censorship over the wildest extravagances of the adventurers.

Personally, I would like to have it both ways. I like to tell stories which require a galactic community of worlds, so that I can indulge my taste for building unusual Earthlike ecospheres. This requires spaceships which travel faster than light (though I am perfectly prepared to believe that in reality faster-than-light travel is quite impossible) and in order to make this plausible I am only too happy to woffle about "hyperspace", shoring up that rather old-hat item of jargon with "wormholes" borrowed from the black hole theorists, and equipping my starships with "stressers" which are supposed to make said wormholes (and also supposed to make my jargon sound that important little bit different from other people's).

On the other hand, as a biologist I am sorely distressed by the cavalier attitude which many sf writers still have to the idea of genetic engineering, and would like to stamp out many of the idiocies which they try to sanction when they invent biotechnological production-lines. ("It's simple, really – we put the sausages into this slot *here*, press this button *here*, and the baby androids fall out *here*, ready for their intelligence-injections.")

As time has gone by I have grown more scrupulous about my own jargon. At one time I was perfectly happy to let my characters wander around with "blasters" which were amazingly destructive and which shared the convenient but mysterious ability of cinematic six-shooters to be fired as often as was needed without reloading. Nowadays I cannot entirely escape niggling doubts about whether the law of conservation of mass-energy is really being observed here, and I find myself wondering about such matters as whether blasters recoil when fired, and what would happen to the energy of the recoil if my characters were in a low-gravity situation. I do not let these things bother me *too* much, mainly because I realise how much less exciting westerns would be if the characters had to reload their guns as often as common sense would require, but I think there are a lot of readers who do appreciate a little bit of conscience in their writers when it comes to thinking up excuses.

If you want to be the kind of sf writer who writes realistic near-future dramas about the exploration of the solar system, then you must do a certain amount of homework. This need not extend as far as cultivating a sophisticated understanding of physics and the contemporary state of the technological arts, because a good deal of work is already done for you, by other sf writers and by popularizers of science. Sf magazines

48

like *Analog* and *New Destinies* carry articles as well as stories, where the game of speculation is played seriously. The popular science magazine *New Scientist* features the marvellous columnist Daedalus, who plays the game for fun, but with an amazingly fertile imagination. Would-be sf writers can find a lot to interest and stimulate them in sources of this kind.

If, on the other hand, you want to be the kind of sf writer whose primary interest is in worldbuilding or time-travelling, and who wants to use imaginary hardware purely for its convenience in getting the characters about the place or for its melodramatic potential in allowing them to fight one another in spectacular fashion, then you can avoid this kind of hard labour. The best advice I can offer is that you can borrow much of what you need from other writers, employing the conventional jargon which sf writers habitually use to describe spaceships, imaginary weapons, and the like. You might want to alter this jargon just the teeniest bit for the sake of propriety, but there is no need to overdo it. If you want to deploy robots, spaceships, laser-weapons, matter-transmitters and artificial intelligences as incidental features of your stories there is no reason why you should not just go ahead, and let other people worry about ways to make those things plausible.

You should keep in mind, though, while borrowing imaginary hardware which other writers have invented, that what you mustn't copy is the ingenious plots which those writers have managed to extrapolate from the devices. You can use the standard sf catalogue of fantastic machines as a construction kit, but you're supposed to make up your own stories.

Even if your command of scientific and pseudoscientific jargon is so weak that you can't even copy it with confidence, you can still fall back on the hoariest stand-by of them all. Let your characters be ordinary people who talk about the parts of the fabulous machines in their environment as "thingumajigs", explaining to each other and to the reader that they haven't a clue how such machines work. Most of your readers will easily be able to sympathise with that, because most of *us* think about bits of the machines which we use in our everyday lives as "thingumajigs" and don't have a clue how the majority of them work.

Chapter Seven

The Language of Science Fiction

Because science fiction writers have to deal with worlds different from our own they are always under pressure to invent new words. One aspect of this process was amply displayed in the last chapter, where I discussed the use of jargon terms in connection with imaginary hardware. In this connection, words made up by sf writers can sometimes make their way into ordinary usage to describe newly-invented real machinery; "robot" is the most obvious example. Other words made up by sf writers can also become fashionable in a wider context – Orwell's *Nineteen Eighty-Four* added "newspeak" and "doublethink" to the language, while Robert Heinlein's *Stranger in a Strange Land* made "grokking" temporarily fashionable. For the most part, though, the words invented by writers remain confined to the books for which they are made up. There they may play a vital part in setting the scene or enhancing plausibility, and if they do their work ineptly they can sometimes ruin a good story.

The problems of naming and describing the operation of imaginary hardware which were discussed in the last chapter usually do not tax linguistic inventiveness very much. Often, sf writers do not have to invent new words to describe imaginary machines and their functions – it is far more common for them to borrow or adapt words which already exist. Even "robot" was not made up from scratch – it was derived by the Czech writer Karel Capek, and came from a Czech word meaning "forced labour". Machines can very often be named simply by saying what it is they are supposed to do, as in the case of real machines like lifts, word-processors and combine harvesters, or hypothetical ones like blasters, matter transmitters and starships. Where ordinary English is insufficient, Latin and Greek roots still remain available for deployment in naming real entities like dynamos, electroencephalographs and television, or hypothetical ones like androids, pedwalks and vidphones.

Where direct description seems inappropriate indirect allusions can often substitute. James Blish was responsible for two such exercises in naming: the Dirac communicator and the spindizzy (the device which lifts and propels the spacefaring cities in his *Cities in Flight* series). In the first instance he co-opts the name of a physicist to describe a device supposedly made possible by a practical application of his theories, in the second he makes uses of a kind of calculated trivialization, such as we engage in when we refer to the family car as our "wheels".

Science fiction continually absorbs the language of science itself, but it does so on a selective basis. Notions which are peripheral in science because they refer to entities whose very existence is dubious may sometimes become important in sf because their literary potential is considerable. Thus tachyons – subatomic particles which travel faster than the speed of light – do not figure large in actual attempts to describe the world, but are very often deployed in sf stories where faster-than-light travel and communication are extremely useful to hypothetical galactic communities.

Would-be sf writers can obtain obvious benefits from becoming well-versed in the language of science. The more scientific terms they can use with authority, the more convincing the jargon of apology which they employ in their "explanations" will be. You can compensate for an ignorance of scientific terminology if you are sufficiently adept in the business of adapting familiar words to the description of imaginary things and processes, but it does make the job harder to do.

There are, however, further problems to do with the inventive use of language which a knowledge of scientific terminology cannot solve, and which are in their way, much more troublesome than the business of concocting mock-scientific explanations. The problem of naming characters and places can become acute, especially if the characters are aliens and the places in question are supposed to have been named by aliens. Even when human characters are involved, futuristic settings may demand changes in the way characters identify themselves.

Even the problems which the sf writer shares with writers of mundane fiction may be exaggerated in sf. The writer who wants to set a story in modern China will have to do some research to find out what kind of names can believably be attached to the Chinese characters who appear in the story, and what words they would use to talk about their tools, clothes and ceremonies, but that research will be limited in scope. The sf writer who looks forward to a cosmopolitan future in which members of all earthly races mingle more freely – so that, for instance, the crew of a starship might be drawn from half a dozen different cultures – is required to have (or to pretend to have) a more wide-ranging knowledge of what kind of names people of different nationalities have. Naming their tools and their clothes may not prove too difficult, but talking about their beliefs and rituals may require further ingenuity in the handling of language. In the early days of sf virtually all human characters were Anglo-American, and the odd token Russian or German was borrowed from a catalogue of stereotypes, but as the genre has grown more sophisticated, expectations have become more rigorous.

This process of sophistication applies to wholly made-up names too. The once-common practice of deriving alien names by spelling common English words backwards nowadays seems unforgivably crude, and it is usually considered that eccentric monosyllables like Tharg and Zork are too silly to be used in serious sf. In addition, it is nowadays expected that the words used to describe an alien culture – including those used to describe objects, beliefs and customs as well as proper names – should sound as if they do come from the *same* language, and should share certain features in the same way that words from different human languages share certain features. There are various strategies for doing this, the most popular being the frequent use of certain non-standard syllables within a set of alien words. Others involve the use of odd combinations of consonants and the deployment of apostrophes to break up the phonetic patterns of supposedly alien words, implying that human tongues are not properly adapted to the business of pronouncing them.

Conscientious sf writers will go so far as to invent rules of pronunciation for their alien names, as James Blish did in *A Case of Conscience*. Those with linguistic training may even go so far as to devise actual grammatical rules for their alien languages, as C. J. Cherryh is prone to do. There is a certain artificiality about this – for instance, when Blish tells us in his pronunciation key that X is to be pronounced K, we may be entitled to wonder why he didn't just write K; after all, the name Xoredeshch is not actually written in an alien alphabet, and the letters used to transcribe the word surely ought to be a phonetic representation. But this is, nevertheless, a functional absurdity – making it difficult for readers to pronounce an alien name is part and parcel of the business of persuading them that the names really are alien.

Having no knowledge of linguistics, and being functionally illiterate in every language but English, I have always found the business of inventing names annoyingly troublesome. I have gone through various phases in which I have employed strategies which range from the utterly stupid to the reasonably adequate, but the task of inventing names for the people and places who will figure in my stories is something which I never look forward to.

For human beings, even where a multicultural context is called for, I generally find telephone directories an adequate source of names; once now and again I scan through one, writing down all the names which catch my eye as being particularly unusual or mellifluous on a "crib sheet" which I can then refer to while writing a story, whenever the need to attach a name to a character crops up. This occasionally lets me down when I need a name of specific nationality, so I have sometimes been forced to borrow from the nation-by-nation guide to authors covered in the *Penguin Companion to European Literature*, and I took care when I visited Japan to bring back a couple of issues of an English-language newspaper for future reference of this kind.

For place-names to be used by humans as they explore the far-flung reaches of the universe the most invaluable resource by far is a knowledge of mythology. The first astronomers who set out to map the sky and name the objects to be found there drew upon their own mythologies, and as modern astronomers have been called upon to expand the lists of heavenly bodies to include those invisible to the naked eye they have followed the same policy. Naming your planets after mythological characters has a certain built-in propriety, and if you know enough to do it cleverly you can often find some mythological character whose plight relates by analogy to some aspect of your plot. Modern sf is replete with such references, and it is not surprising that many writers go in for the wholesale plunder of mythological motifs in formulating their plots. Roger Zelazny tends to do this most extravagantly, but it is surprising how often one finds the careful and highly scientific extrapolation of the hard sf writer coupled with romantic metaphors and allusions drawn from mythology – there are many examples to be found in the work of Poul Anderson.

For these reasons I keep among the reference books which are ready to hand while I am writing Tripp's *Handbook of Classical Mythology*, the *Everyman Dictionary of Non-Classical Mythology* and a *Larousse Encyclopedia of Mythology*. I use them constantly as sources of names and motifs to decorate my plots.

Alien names are difficult to derive in quantity, and I have always found them very difficult to produce – I envy those writers whose linguistic skills allow them to put up a more convincing show. I have at various times past compiled crib sheets of "alien" names derived from the index to the *Times* atlas, and from abbreviated versions of the Latin names in the index of an encyclopedia of animal life. Neither of these served me particularly well, and the crib sheets out of which I actually got most mileage over the years were compiled from horse-racing form books (there are a few of my early novels where virtually all the characters and places are named after racehorses). These days, alas, the dominance of Arab owners is importing a distinct cultural bias into the naming of racehorses, and one does have to worry slightly about the possibility of unknowingly using a word whose actual meaning, in whatever foreign language it comes from, is ridiculously inappropriate.

At one stage in my early career I made up exotic surnames

for characters who figured in eccentric space operas by combining ordinary words, often thereby giving some indication of the character of the person described, somewhat after the fashion of early Victorian novels in which good men might be called Allworthy and vicars surnamed Kenemall. Although I only did this in stories which were already artificialised (as, for instance, when I rewrote the Iliad and the Odyssey as the first two parts of a trilogy of space operas) it now seems to me to be a ploy which failed to come off. I am unlikely to write any more stories whose heroes bear such unlikely surnames as Stargazer and Stormwind (which I now recall with slight embarrassment), and I would not recommend the method for use in sf. It is, of course, rather more commonplace in fantasy and it might also be noteworthy that a character named Luke Skywalker was deemed entirely acceptable as the hero of the film *Star Wars*.

The problem of choosing names for use in sf stories may seem fairly trivial, unworthy of the space which I am giving to it, but in fact the atmosphere and effectiveness of a story can depend very heavily on the names which are used there, and on the language which is used in describing exotic environments. The more exotic the story-setting is, the more important it is to find names which sound appropriate. Clark Ashton Smith, who produced the most exotic fantasy stories ever written, enhanced the bizarrerie of the events which he described by inventing extraordinarily exotic names and using a language full of sonorous archaisms. Some readers do find it difficult to read stories in which such nouns as eidolon and mithridate, and such adjectives as fulvous and tenebrous, continually recur, but their use does give the stories a particular ambience. There is a certain undeniable integrity in naming the world's last continent Zothique, or a female vampire Morthylla, or a sorceror Malygris, though there may be some justice in Smith's detractors feeling that even an element of comedy cannot add propriety to a title like "The Weird of Avoosl Wuthoqquan".

Some fine examples of deft naming by a language-conscious sf writer can be found in the work of Brian Aldiss, my favourite being *The Malacia Tapestry* (malacia is a kind of pathological softening of the tissues, a perfect metaphor for the kind of degeneracy featured in the book). A certain acquaintance with words not in common usage, especially ones which sound nice, can be a great asset to the would-be sf writer in search of appropriate names.

When they are employed crudely, stylistic devices of this kind can fall flat. Archaisms can easily grate on the ear if writer and reader are not in sympathy with one another, though of course tastes in these matters do vary. For myself, I do not think Edgar Rice Burroughs sounds any more stylish when he refers to muscles as "thews" and grass as "sward", nor am I prepared to be impressed by the not-so-cunning way in which the enemy alien races in Edward E. Smith's space operas tend to be named after expressions of disgust (Eich! Ploor! etc.)

It is, unfortunately, a great deal easier to parody sf nomenclature than it is to do the job convincingly. This can be to the advantage of writers of comedy sf, who generally have a far easier time when it comes to naming things. The comedy writer can jump head first into all the pitfalls which threaten the serious writer, and should not find it too difficult to come up with suitable absurdities. Even parody has a certain artistry to it, however, and tastes in humour vary even more widely than tastes in archaisms. I must admit that discovering a character named Zaphod Beeblebrox does not in itself make me fall about laughing, though it does seem to have that effect on some people, and the fact that it does should serve to make sf and fantasy writers beware of offering easy ammunition to parodists.

A story which has too great a density of made-up words (especially if they are difficult to pronounce) can become difficult to read. There are numerous sf novels which need glossaries, and some readers find it irritating to be forced to flick back and forth between text and glossary in order to be able to follow what is happening. Editors unused to the conventions of sf sometimes worry unduly about this – the editor who was entrusted with my novel *The Empire of Fear* wanted to cut out many of the words which I had borrowed from the Yoruba language for use in the part of the book which is set in Africa, and also wanted to remove the "thees" and "thous" which I had used in the dialogue (not inappropriately, given that the novel is set in an alternative seventeenth century). I felt that the editor was under-estimating the willingness of readers to tackle text in which unusual words are used, but it *is* necessary for writers to think carefully about the way they are using their made-up words, and about the business of introducing them to the reader. Readers will bear with a writer who is setting an exotic scene, and most are perfectly happy to come across words which they don't already know, but it is part of the writer's job to stay within the limits of that tolerance and to make things as easy for the reader as practicality will allow.

There are more subtle points to be made about the language of sf, which go much deeper into the matter than the simple questions which I have so far discussed. One at least has been interesting enough to become a subject of discussion in essays and sf writers' workshops. This is the fact that the knowledge that a narrative is fantastic may cast into ambiguity certain common phrases which, in mundane narrative, can only be used metaphorically. For instance, when a mundane narrative refers to a character "losing her heart", the reader instantly translates this as a reference to infatuation, but in a fantastic narrative characters really *can* lose their hearts.

One finds calculated literalization of metaphors in many fairy tales – it is common in stories where people are granted wishes, which then turn out more literally (and more unfortunately) than they intended. Some common metaphors actually come from fantastic stories – as when we speak, for instance, of the Midas touch or a fairy godmother. Literalization of the fairy tale type can be found abundantly in Piers Anthony's fantasies, which feature a series of awful puns based in common metaphors, and there are sf stories whose plots are derived from the same kind of wordplay – Isaac Asimov's "Little Lost Robot", for instance, describes how a logical robot responds to a careless instruction to "Get lost!"

This extra dimension of ambiguity is something which needs to be drawn to the attention of would-be writers, partly because they must beware of creating unintended double meanings by accident, and partly because it is something which can occasionally be used to telling effect. Serious sf stories often use such acquired ambiguity as a stylistic device, and it is not uncommon to find stories which start with such a reprocessed metaphor. Thus, for instance, Vonda McIntyre's *Superluminal* begins with the non-metaphorical sentence: "She gave up her heart quite willingly." My own story "The Engineer and the Executioner" begins with a character protesting to the effect that his life is being threatened. The statement is deliberately deceptive because the reader quickly realises that he is a genetic engineer, and that it is the life-system which he has created which is under threat rather than his own life – a reversal of meaning which is then ironically re-inverted by the plot, in the course of which the life-system is saved (and the Earth doomed) by the engineer's suicidal self-sacrifice.

The way in which language is used to construct a sciencefictional narrative – to describe a world other than the one to which the language in question is specifically adapted – raises issues which are interesting enough to warrant very serious philosophical examination. It would be inappropriate in a book like this to venture into these deeper waters, but I would urge writers who have a particular interest in such matters to seek out various essays on the subject by Samuel R. Delany – some, including "About 5,750 Words" and "Thickening the Plot" can be found in his collection *The Jewel-Hinged Jaw*, and a minute phrase-by-phrase analysis of a sf story by Thomas M. Disch, exploring the devices employed in it, is featured in *The American Shore*. Would-be writers who are interested in the theoretical aspects of sf writing as well as the practical issues involved will probably find these books, as I did, quite fascinating.

Chapter Eight

Characterization in Science Fiction

All stories have characters, and the problems of characterization are common to all kinds of fiction-writing. This is something to which most books on writing pay a great deal of attention, because many literary critics feel that literary merit is very largely determined by the ability to create characters who seem to "live and breathe". Many writers and critics believe that the best ambition of the novelist is to describe in the most convincing possible way the "stream of consciousness" which constitutes the mental life of its characters. There is a sense, too, in which our own actual characters – our real selves – are developed in the same way that a writer develops an imaginary character; we are, as it were, constantly engaged in constructing the narratives of our own lives.

To a large extent, the problems facing the sf writer who must create characters are similar to those which face writers of mundane fiction – most of the viewpoint characters in sf are, after all, human beings not fundamentally different from the characters in other kinds of stories. There are, however, certain special problems of characterization which arise because of the particular nature of sf, and which require consideration here.

The most obvious problem which sf throws up is that it contains a much wider range of characters than mundane fiction. Some of the intelligent actors in sf are by definition *not* human, and the question of how to go about making such individuals into "believable characters" can be a very vexing one.

All writers, of course, have to characterize people who are significantly different from themselves. Stories by men have to contain women, and vice versa. The problems which face a female writer who wishes to paint a convincing portrait of an alcoholic priest or a businessman in the throes of mid-life crisis are by no means inconsiderable. Even so, such problems might in the final analysis be reduced to matters of observation. She may well number several businessmen among her acquaintances, and even if she knows no alcoholic priests she may know an alcoholic or two and a priest or two. If not, she can always watch TV, where real-life examples will occasionally appear, eager to explain their predicament to documentary-makers. The would-be writer of mundane fiction can be advised by writers of guidebooks to go out into the world to watch people, to listen attentively to conversations and memorise mannerisms of behaviour, and that is usually what they *are* advised to do.

Such advice cannot help the sf writer who wants to offer a persuasive account of the personality of a sentient computer, or the psychology of a man radically altered by manipulation of his genes. When the sf writer asks how the attitudes of an alien whose species is descended from catlike predators are likely to differ from those of a species like ours, descended from ape-like omnivores, the problem must be solved by reasoning, not by observation.

Nor is this the full extent of the problems which the sf writer must face. The characterization of human beings is also much more problematic in sf than it is in mundane fiction. Many of the tricks which writers of mundane fiction use to make their readers feel that they really *know* the people in the stories involve showing the ways that those characters operate in familiar and stereotyped situations. Getting to know people – real or imaginary – is not an exercise in abstract psychology but an exercise in social ecology. Knowing what someone is like is a matter of knowing how they relate to their environment; we can quickly get a sense of the particular personality of a fictitious character if we can observe his or her idiosyncratic response to a situation which we already understand in terms of norms and customs. But in sf the environment of the story usually does not have those situations in it.

The strategies of characterization which adequately serve the mundane novelist will work in a near-future story of catastrophe or scientific discovery, but cannot be expected to work as well in a story which launches its readers into the far future, forcing them to set aside all their expectations about norms, customs and everyday situations. Writers of such stories must make their characters interact with environments which are unfamiliar, and this makes it much more difficult for them to make their characters "convincing" or "believable". Indeed, the attempt to foist upon people who are supposedly living two hundred years from now the foibles, verbal habits and moral outlooks of the present day is rather absurd. There are no characters in fiction who seem more ridiculous to us than the ones which writers of the nineteenth century invented to populate their visions of our times.

It has become a commonplace of literary criticism that sf writers are bad at characterization. It is one of the most frequent arguments used by those hostile to the genre to denigrate it, and one often hears apologists for the genre admitting and lamenting the fact. Alas, it could not be otherwise. Some sf writers are undoubtedly not as good at characterization as they could be, even within the limits permitted by the nature of the stories which they have to tell, but the simple fact is that no matter how clever they were, they could only match the performance of the best writers of mundane fiction by placing severe limitations on the kinds of imaginary worlds they put into their fiction.

What kind of things you can and ought to do in the attempt to create your characters, therefore, will depend in large measure on the setting of your story. The closer to home your scenarios are, the easier it will be to devise situations whose purpose is to reveal the crucial aspects of your characters' personalities. A convenient and oft-quoted rule of thumb to bear in mind in establishing personalities is "show, don't tell" – if you want to establish that your character is mean you can do it far more convincingly by including a scene where he acts with striking meanness than simply by stating that he is mean. (This is a rule of which I knew nothing in my younger days, and though my first published novel has as its central character a coward forced by circumstances to behave heroically I failed to include an early scene where he actually behaves in a cowardly fashion.)

This rule of thumb can still be applied in some very exotic

circumstances, but the stranger the setting is, the less complex the demonstration can be, and the tendency is to produce characters each of whom has a single dominant character trait. One can see this in fairy stories, where characters are often no more than embodiments of a single quality. The rule can also work, in a rough and ready fashion, to show off the significant traits of characters who are not human – indeed, to demonstrate and dramatise their non-humanity. Thus, stories which feature robots often include scenes which show the robot reacting to a situation in a way that no human being would, usually demonstrating lack of emotion. Here, though, we really are in a world of "one dimensional" characters.

Robots are, for the most part, less than human in terms of the complexity of their character. Their characterization is therefore negative, in the sense that the writer mainly wants to show off things that they don't do. Even super-intelligent robots in sf tend to be quaintly simple-minded. Characterization in sf is very often accomplished by showing that the entity in question lacks something that human beings normally have; I am sometimes astonished by the number of stories which take it for granted that anyone or anything which is intelligent but not human would lack emotions. The most famous example of this kind of characterization by emotional deprivation is, of course, *Star Trek*'s utterly logical Mr. Spock.

Less-than-human characters figure in other kinds of fiction as well as sf. Childrens' stories very often feature animals which are characterized by "anthropomorphization" – treating them as though they have self-awareness and an ability to think in words. This can be done in a clever and reasonably sophisticated way, by taking strict account of the lifestyle of the real animals in question, as Richard Adams attempts to do with the rabbits in *Watership Down*. Readers are very willing to be "taken in" by this kind of strategy, and in fact find no difficulty at all in identifying with non-human characters. You can easily check this by watching the audience react to such celebrated tear-jerking films as *Bambi* and *E.T.* Indeed, many readers are content to be *more* sympathetic to talking animals and aliens, because one of the things which can easily be left out in this characterization-by-censorship is human nastiness.

The problems involved in creating a character who is *more* than human are, of course, of a very different order. There is a certain logical impossibility involved when a human writer attempts to portray a mental superman – someone supposedly much more intelligent than himself. That logical impossibility has not stopped writers from trying, and there has never been any shortage of sf writers who were convinced that they knew exactly how a mental superman would regard his fellow men – H. G. Wells and L. Ron Hubbard, to name but two. Novels which attempt to describe in some detail the personality and experiences of superhuman beings have the inbuilt appeal of all wish-fulfilment fantasies, though, and this helps readers to go along with the gag. The most flamboyant attempt to do it can be found in Thomas M. Disch's book *Camp Concentration.* (It is worth noting that the cunning way to write about the augmentation of intelligence is to use as protagonist an animal or a moron, whose elevation need not involve the acquisition of unimaginable powers, as in Daniel Keyes' classic *Flowers for Algernon*, which draws heavily on the tear-jerk effect as well as the wish-fulfilment hook.)

Just as there is a paradox in the attempt by a human writer to characterize the superhuman, so there is a paradox in the human writer's attempt to characterize the alien. In the vast majority of sf stories the aliens are no more than people in fancy costumes or sub-human monsters. The exceptions tend to be those stories which present aliens as fundamentally inexplicable – the cardinal example is Stanislaw Lem's *Solaris* – but there is a sense in which this cannot be regarded as characterization at all.

Nevertheless, there is a sensible way to tackle the question of how to characterize the other-than-human. It is basically a compare-and-contrast exercise of the same kind as trying to figure out how a self-aware rabbit might see things. Scientific essayists have occasionally tackled projects of this kind – Julian Huxley's *Essays of a Biologist* includes the classic "Philosophic Ants", in which he tried to imagine what the world-view of an ant might be like, taking as premises what biologists have discovered about the way ants communicate and the way they are organised into a hive society. J. B. S. Haldane, in the title essay of his collection *Possible Worlds*, did the same thing, albeit briefly, for the barnacle.

Sf writers can only design aliens by comparing them to life-forms we already know about. Our knowledge of biology becomes a kind of identikit with which we build images of the alien – and we then have the criteria with which we can build a kind of world-view. Recently, writers have begun extending this kind of "hypothetical existentialism" to the traditional figures of mythology; there have been several interesting exercises in vampire existentialism, of which the best is Suzy McKee Charnas's *The Vampire Tapestry*. Charnas very carefully develops the notion that from the vampire's point of view, humans are prey, and that he cannot regard them in any other way than humans regard cattle or sheep. Sf writers attribute characteristics to aliens in the same way; and when they draw on analogies between their aliens and animals – as Anne McCaffrey does by basing her dragons on horses, or C. J. Cherryh in her portraits of catlike aliens in the *Chanur* series – they can exploit the emotional attitudes to those animals which their readers already possess, in order to make them care about the aliens in question.

All this is, in a sense, cheating. We are characterizing the alien by denying its essential alienness. But alien beings are really only interesting to us because they *can* be compared and contrasted with us – because they can make us reconsider our attitudes to one another, and to the other inhabitants of the world we live in. It is a sad fact that the other people who share the world with us include some who are more alien to us than any alien we could ever invent, but it *is* a fact. There are other human beings, who could easily be our parents or our children, whose attitudes and experiences we cannot and never could understand. We call them "mad" or "perverted", but what we mean is that we cannot see things as they see them. We cannot understand why they cannot simply snap out of their dementia, or cease to feel the impulse which tempts them sexually to molest small children; in other words, we cannot characterize them

– we cannot make them "live and breathe" like our favourite characters in books, even though they manifestly do live and breathe in the real world.

The only advice which I can offer with reference to the thorny question of how to go about science fictional characterization is to urge that writers should cheat as cleverly as they can. Given that the task is impossible, one can only look for resources which will help to fake it. I have already noted in chapter 5 that sf writers designing alien societies often turn to the reports of anthropologists on the customs and world-views of the many tribes they have studied. It is from such reports that we can best judge the limits of everyday human behaviour, and hence the limits which determine whether our readers will be able to identify with and sympathise with our hypothetical aliens.

Would-be sf writers should not worry too much about the fact that their aliens can only be humans in disguise, or at best akin to the talking animals and giants in fairy stories. After all, the purpose of writing sf stories is not to design "real" aliens any more than the purpose of fairy stories is to tell us what talking animals and giants would "really" be like. Imaginary beings provide us with ingenious ways of learning more about ourselves. We see more clearly when we learn "to see ourselves as others see us", and we can gain improved understanding by constructing a whole series of hypothetical others whose viewpoints we can adopt and with whom we might compare ourselves. Sf writers, who have brought into being a vaster number and a greater range of hypothetical others than was ever dreamed of before, have made a worthwhile contribution to the human understanding of human beings.

Although what I have said above is to be taken seriously, it is worth remembering that writers can get away with paying very scant attention to characterization if they so wish. It is at least arguable that most people who try to teach the business of writing, or give advice about it, pay altogether too much attention to characterization because of the way that literary critics judge the merit of novelists. It should be noted that this is just a matter of doctrine, which has nothing much to do with the writer's ability to please the reader.

The majority of readers seem only to want a point of

identification within a story – one character in whom they can be interested. It is not necessary for them to get to know that character intimately, and it may actually make things more difficult for them if they are told a great deal about the character's idiosyncracies. Over-characterization can make a story just as stodgy as over-description, and though some effort in establishing the personalities of minor characters is always necessary, there is no need to take elaborate pains over it if all you want to do is tell an entertaining story. Critics tend to be rather hard on those writers who take no pains at all with characterization, putting their best efforts into the construction of a fast-paced plot, but readers are often very fond of such books. In my opinion, there is no need to feel guilty about writing stories which require only elementary characterization.

Chapter Nine

Plotting a Science Fiction Story

The over-elaborate attention which most teachers of writing give to characterization is usually complemented by a marked indifference to plotting. It is almost as if the business of constructing a plot were considered too vulgar to warrant consideration by the truly literary, although it does seem to be the case that the majority of readers are more interested in the plots of the stories which they read than in any other aspect of them.

One objection which teachers of creative writing have to the business of plotting is that it is something which can be summarised very easily. A description of how an author goes about the business of characterization might be longer than the story, but an account of the plot is always shorter. Worse still, plots are very often conventional, reducible to formulas. Thus, the plot of very many detective stories can be summed up as: somebody gets murdered; the detective gathers all the evidence and uses ingenious powers of logical deduction to determine who did it. The plot of most romances is just as simple: nice girl meets ruggedly handsome man; their attitudes and circumstances seem bound to keep them apart, but they eventually get together, realising at last that this is the one thing which will make their lives worthwhile.

The fact that one can reduce whole genres of fiction to fairly simple formulas seems to most literary critics to be a blanket certificate of worthlessness. After all, one of the qualities which great works of literature are supposed to possess is originality, and the originality which simply produces endless variations on a single theme seems substandard. Would-be writers, however, might care to bear in mind the fact that formularistic plots do work. In spite of their predictability they command the attention and the affection of many readers. People who do not care for them often speak scornfully of the kind of romances published by firms like Mills & Boon, mocking the rigid formula to which they are produced, but that derision does not prevent the millions of people who value the experience of reading them from buying and enjoying them.

At first glance, sf appears to be much less formularistic than most genres. Sf has many different settings, and the range of potential happenings in an sf story is much greater than in any other kind of fiction. Nevertheless, its plots do often follow familiar patterns, and there are good reasons for this. It is action and suspense which make stories attractive and exciting to the great majority of readers, and action and suspense are generated by plots. The plot is, in a way, the skeleton of a story, upon which the literary flesh is built. It may be the literary flesh which is responsible for making a story distinctive and beautiful, just as it is actual flesh which makes people distinctive and beautiful, but it is the skeleton which gives the story structure, strength, and power of movement, and if it is to do that, it needs to be built according to a certain set plan. Plots vary, just as the skeletons of birds, fish and mammals vary, but these are variations on a theme.

I would strongly advise would-be writers not to despise plot formulas, and to make what productive use of them they can. Some of the best-known sf writers in America worked for the Scott Meredith Literary Agency at a time when the agency advised would-be pulp writers ambitious to become its clients to use a standard formula. The formula ran along the following lines: begin by establishing a sympathetic lead character who is faced with an urgent problem, then show how his (or her) preliminary attempts to cope with the problem make things worse, before he ultimately contrives by his own efforts to bring about a solution.

It is certainly true that there have been countless good stories written which do not fit this formula, but there is no doubt that it is a very useful formula which is capable of generating lots of good stories. It is arguable that nothing in the formula is absolutely necessary to the production of an effective story, but each element does serve a purpose. If your lead character is not sympathetic, you may alienate some readers; if there is no urgency about what he has to do your story if likely to lack pace and suspense; if he is not at first frustrated the story may seem too facile; if a solution is not obtained as a result of his own efforts the reader identifying with him will get less satisfaction out of the climax.

Writers should never become slaves to formulas of this kind, but they can be invaluable crutches, especially for beginners, and they deserve to be taken seriously. They do not undermine or seek to take over the processes of creativity; what we mean by an "original" plot is not one which avoids the formula but one which sets up a particularly ingenious or unusual problem for which the characters will ultimately discover a particularly elegant or ironic solution. The capacity which sf offers for unexpected happenings certainly opens up much more space for surprising events and surprising endings, but if these do not become part of the hero's frustrations and achievements as mapped out by the Scott Meredith plot formula the reader may simply feel cheated – a story where the central problem is solved by dragging in some entirely new factor (what the jargon calls a *deus ex machina*) usually does not work very well.

What I have seen of the first efforts of would-be sf writers (and it is certainly supported by my own early experiences) suggests to me that it is regrettably easy to get carried away by a particular image or idea, so that one writes down a description of a bizarre event or a strange environment without paying any attention at all to the question of what kind of plot would make the best use of the idea. It is true, as I have said, that a sf story usually has an idea rather than a character as its focal point, but that does not mean that the idea can support a narrative on its own. The lens which brings the idea into focus is the plot of the story, and the hardest work a writer has to do – far harder than actually thinking up ideas to use – is in shaping his story to display his idea to best advantage. Providing an effective plot is the most fundamental aspect of that shaping.

Some writers do tend to be dismissive about the work of plotting, observing that there are only a handful of "basic plots". Robert Heinlein wrote a celebrated article offering advice to would-be sf writers, in which he claimed that there were only three: "Boy Meets Girl", "The Little Tailor" and "The Man Who Learned Better". It needs only a slight adjustment of perspective to recognise that all three are variants of a single theme: the Success Story. The first features success in love, the second success in a career, the third success in coming to terms with the way of the world. One might add that there *are* other kinds of success story: "Who-Done-It?" features puzzle-solving success: "How The Hell Do I Get Out Of *This* Mess?" is the escaped-threat success story (which features very prominently in horror fiction). One might also point out that each of these plots has a corresponding "anti-plot" or "tragic variant" in which success is not attained.

Reduction of this kind should not, however, be interpreted as a dismissal of the problems of plotting as something unimportant or facile; it is really a matter of pointing out what we mean by the word "plot". What this kind of argument says is that the plot of a story relates to the projects which the characters in a story have, and to whether those projects will come to a successful conclusion or not. There are exactly as many "basic plots" as there are basic needs of human existence: the elementary factors involved in surviving and thriving. That is why I observed in an earlier chapter that a useful method of trying to find a plot which will display your idea is to ask who might get hurt if the world were changed in the way that you imagine.

What plot formulas tend to leave out, curiously, is the reason why plots are capable of gripping the attention of readers and getting them "involved" in the story – which is perhaps the main reason why such a thing as fiction exists at all. What both the Scott Meredith formula and the Heinlein account of basic plots fail to mention, though it is in a sense the very essence of plotting, is the notion of moral order.

The world in which we live appears to have no inbuilt moral order. As St. Matthew and everyone else has observed, rain falls on the just and the unjust alike. The wicked are no more likely to get struck down by lightning or by cancer than those who live like saints. This conflicts with our moral sensibilities; we feel that the wicked *deserve* to suffer misfortune and that the good *deserve* to be rewarded. It is because the real world perversely fails to punish the wicked and tragically fails to reward the good that people have speculated about an afterlife in which this failure will be decisively rectified.

The world of a story, however, differs from the real world in that the writer is there to guide the hand of providence. He has the power to reward his good characters and punish his wicked ones, and if he does not do so it is because he has *chosen* not to do so. Chance plays no role in fiction – or, if it does (if, for instance, a writer decided to let the outcome of his story depend on the throw of a dice) it is only because the writer deliberately abandons his power of choice.

What happens in a story, therefore, cannot help but have some kind of moral significance. This is why the success of the hero of a story is uplifting: that success is the reward for all his cleverness and virtue. Readers love to see the villain of a story come unstuck and perish horribly, not because they are sadistic, but because they recognise the moral propriety of his extinction.

This is why people are not only willing but eager to read what is essentially the same plot over and over again – it is a ritual assertion of moral principle. This is also why most people prefer "upbeat" (morally proper) endings to "downbeat" ones (where the good do not receive the full measure of their apparent entitlement). Downbeat stories – tragedies – are intended to make us uncomfortable, by sharpening our awareness of the failings of the world we live in, and many people feel that they are all too sharply aware of that already.

The plots of sf cannot help but be similar in kind to the plots of other kinds of fiction. The characters with whom we identify, whether they be human or unhuman, may have projects which are distinctive in detail – boldly going where no man has gone before – but they inevitably have the same kind of moral weight as the projects adopted by characters in Greek drama, Shakespearean tragedy, western films and romantic novels. It is true that our notions of what ought to count as good and what ought to count as evil are subject to negotiation, varying from society to society and over time, but the *nature* of moral questions does not alter, and there is a substantial cross-cultural consensus about the fundamentals of good and evil.

Having said this, though, it must also be said that there are some particular moral issues which are addressed more easily and more frequently by sf than by any other kind of fiction – and this is the main reason why I believe that sf is an interesting, worthwhile and important species of fiction. There are two issues which seem to me to be of cardinal importance.

One moral issue which sf writers often address in their plotting, but which writers in other genres rarely touch, is the question of how we should actually constitute a "moral community". To what kind of entities do we owe moral consideration?

In the real world, and hence in mundane fiction, this is an easy issue to evade, the simplest move being to say that we owe moral consideration only to other people – this still leaves room for painful disputes about animal rights and the rights of embryos, but it narrows down the discussion to a point where we often do not inquire deeply into the underlying logic of our decisions. Only in sf can we produce moral dramas asking whether an animal with augmented intelligence, or an alien, or a sentient machine is worthy of moral consideration. By asking such hypothetical questions we can actually get to the heart of the question of what it is about an entity which entitles it to be the object of moral concern. There are some sf stories, like Robert Heinlein's "Jerry was a Man" and Vercors' novel *Borderline*, in which the case is actually argued out in a hypothetical court of law.

A second issue which is implicit in the plots of very many sf stories, but much less obvious outside sf, is the question of what constitutes "progress". It is not only individual people who have projects in which they may succeed or fail; people band together into groups, ranging from families and clubs to professions and nations, and these groups take on projects of their own in order to serve the needs and interests of the individuals within them. It makes sense to ask whether the whole human race ought to have a project, what that project should be, and what the chances of succeeding in it are. These are the questions which are involved in the concept of progress; they are questions which surface explicitly in many sf stories, and which are tacitly at stake in many others.

The resolution of a plot in a sf story is almost always concerned with more than the fates of the characters who appear in it; the story usually requires that its resolution bears upon the fate of the hypothetical world which is, in a sense, the true "hero" of the story. Sf is not just about good and bad people who may or may not get their just desserts; it is about worlds which might be better or worse than ours, and the prospects of changing them.

It is still possible to make a career as a sf writer by writing costume drama, in which the only things at stake in your plots will be whether or not the protagonist makes a fortune, gets his own back on the bad guys and marries the prettiest girl around. There is a lot of that kind of costume drama in fantasy, too, though it should be pointed out that the best fantasy also has a particular moral significance of its own – indeed, the chief attraction of Secondary World fantasy is that it can bring moral issues into much sharper focus than fiction about the real world usually permits, often with a literalised conflict between Good and Evil. I think that sf's handling of the moral issues with which it is most often concerned entitles it to much more serious consideration from literary historians and literary critics than it has so far received. It is interesting to note that sf plots and situations have come to play a significant part in modern philosophical arguments which try to grapple with such questions as how we ought to define a moral community.

Science fictional costume drama, which employs the Scott Meredith plot formula in its crudest form, concerned only with the fate of the particular characters in the story, can be exciting to write and to read. I would say to all would-be sf writers, though, that if you want to produce *real* sf then you must bear in mind while you are designing your plots that larger issues – up to and including the fate of the human race – can and should be a matter for consideration. The fate of a hypothetical society transformed by its adoption of a particular technology is something that you might require your readers to care about as much as, and perhaps more than, the fate of the particular individuals who figure in your story. All the best sf possesses this grander moral vision, though doctrinaire literary critics sometimes do not recognise it as a virtue, and sometimes regard it as a poor substitute for "good characterization".

In my own work I have not always practised what I have preached in this book (though I have tried to be honest in identifying my failures). With respect to my plotting, however, I have from the very beginning of my career tried to incorporate these larger issues in my work, even in the crudest of my works. The stories which I have written of which I am most proud – "And He Not Busy Being Born . . .", *Sexual Chemistry*, *The Growth of the House of Usher* and *The Empire of Fear* – are all consciously and directly addressed to the question of what would count as a better world than the one we now live in, and I made every effort to be clever, original and provocative in formulating their plots around that question.

Although critics have sometimes claimed that I have a rather downbeat view of things (which I deny) I think that I am on safe ground in claiming that my story "Sexual Chemistry" not only has a happy ending, but that it has the *only* truly happy ending to which a science fiction story should aspire. At the risk of spoiling the surprise for readers who have yet to encounter it, the last two lines of the story are:

They lived happily ever after.
And so did everybody else.

Chapter Ten

Playfulness and Seriousness in Science Fiction

What I wrote in the last chapter about plotting sf stories has already introduced some fairly heavy discussion of the seriousness of sf, and in the interests of balance I think we ought to move on directly to some comments about the playfulness of sf. We will still be concerned as we do so with matters of plotting, but plotting of a rather different kind.

What I said about the involvement of sf plots with the idea of progress follows on logically from sf's representation of itself as a genre dedicated to sensible extrapolation and the exploration of real possibilities. As I have admitted before, though, that representation is at best only a half-truth. There are certain kinds of story which are accepted as perfectly normal varieties of sf, though they deal with notions which are essentially impossible.

The archetype of this kind of story is the time-paradox story, whose simplest version describes a person going back into his own past to murder his grandfather, thus ensuring that he never gets born and thus cannot go back in time to shoot his grandfather. It might seem that the reasonable conclusion to draw from consideration of a case like this is that time travel into the past is impossible, and thus cannot figure in a serious sf story about real possibilities, but in fact the attitude of sf writers has been very different. Paradoxes have an aesthetic appeal of their own, and sf writers have been continually drawn back to time paradox stories in order to explore this aesthetic potential to the full.

Some writers have tried to imagine ways in which the universe might be arranged so as to prevent the paradox becoming pernicious, defying the best efforts of the time-traveller to disrupt it. This kind of thinking underlies those stories in which people can only travel into those bits of past time where they cannot meet themselves. Others, however, have blithely exploited time paradoxes to tie their plots in impossible but intriguing knots. There are many stories in which travel into the past initiates chains of causation which form "closed loops" – the most famous example is Robert Heinlein's "All You Zombies", in which the central character's travels in time permit him to become his own father and mother, thus making him (in his own estimation) the only person in the world who can satisfactorily account for his existence.

Stories of this kind can address serious issues – Gregory Benford's *Timescape* tries to take seriously the metaphysical question of whether the universe can, in fact, accommodate paradoxes. For the most part, though, they are exercises in game-playing where the reader's pleasure comes from being surprised by the author's ingenuity. There are many other sf stories which use sf's standard catalogue of ideas to produce similarly ingenious inversions of perspective, producing stories which are more like jokes than serious attempts to plumb the depths of moral philosophy or anticipate what opportunities and hazards future technology may bring.

Young readers are sometimes attracted to sf by the sheer cleverness of the "twists in the tail" which many sf stories have. Mundane stories too can often derive their effectiveness from the production of crucial alterations in perspective in the last few lines, but there are limitations in the kinds of inversion which can occur and most readers quickly get used to them – everyone who regularly watches the TV programme *Tales of the Unexpected* soon learns to reason along the lines that whatever the storyteller is encouraging us to believe must be false, and that the truth of the matter is likely to be the negative image of the appearance. Sf, however, permits a much wider range of possibility than mundane fiction, and thus much greater scope for surprising inversions of expectation.

It is this kind of story which many would-be writers of sf long to write; unfortunately, it is also this kind of story which is most vulnerable to the criticism that "it's already been done!" It is, alas, becoming more and more difficult for anyone to think up an original twist for a time paradox story, and the person most likely to figure one out is not the young writer who comes to the problem afresh but the old hand who has read all the others. What the new writer thinks of as a brilliant inspiration is only too likely to have occurred to a hundred equally clever new writers, who similarly did not realise that Isaac Asimov got in first way back in 1941. I would not wish to discourage new writers from exercising their ingenuity in trying to think up gimmicks of this kind, but they would be over-optimistic were they to expect such ingenuity to supply them with a ready supply of saleable stories. The sf writer of today cannot live by twists in the tail alone.

Sf's vocabulary of ideas easily lends itself to other kinds of exercises in absurdity. Another kind of playfulness which is common in sf is a delight in bizarrerie for its own sake, and sf novels do lend themselves to witty embellishment by the inclusion of weird life-forms and eccentric machines, which may serve no function in the story but which are amusing in themselves. Comic sf goes in very heavily for these witty asides – Douglas Adams' galactic hitch-hiker books are composed almost entirely of them – but they also crop up in abundance in colourful adventure stories of the kind which Jack Vance writes. The comic fantasies which Piers Anthony and Terry Pratchett write also offer abundant scope for playfulness of this kind, and humorous fantasy seems to be enjoying great success in the marketplace nowadays – probably because a glut of earnest and sometimes pompous fantasies has prepared the way for readers to enjoy parodies thereof.

Writers who intend to go in for this kind of work have two linked problems which they must face. The first is the problem of combining episodes which are effectively self-contained sketches into any kind of overall scheme or plot. The writer who solves this problem by making do with the barest skeleton on an overall plot to link his funny scenes together then has the corollary problem of maintaining imaginative fertility. Without the pace and suspense of a plot it becomes very important that each new item of bizarre incident should be at least as interesting as the last; otherwise the story loses its impetus.

I shudder to think how many people must start out to write a story of this kind, emboldened by the fact that they do not have to do much in the way of preparatory planning, only to find that they run out of good enough ideas long before decency permits them to reach a conclusion. Paradoxical as it may seem, writing a story without a plot is much harder than writing a story with one, and producing a long string of frothy absurdities is very much more difficult than it may appear to be. Easy reading is usually the product of hard writing, and serious writers tend to hold their form rather better than comic ones over the course of a career.

It is important to emphasize that playfulness and seriousness are not necessarily opposites between which the writer has to choose. The two can be combined, and frequently are – as satirists readily demonstrate, one can make serious argumentative points while being far from deadly earnest in one's manner. The writing of action-adventure stories is basically a playful enterprise which can readily be approached in a breezy and light-hearted fashion, but there is no reason at all why the dangers which threaten the hero and the rewards which are there for him to win cannot be matters of some importance. It will probably help your reader to care more if they *are* matters of some importance, because there comes a time in the career of most readers when they can no longer get excited about one more monster which stumbles arbitrarily into the path of the hero, or whether the Martian princess is to be safely delivered from one more in an interminable series of threatened rapes.

The most successful writers of sf are those who most cleverly integrate playfulness and seriousness. Their plots are authentically science fictional plots, dealing with those questions of moral order which mundane plots cannot reach, but they are plots which have an essential zest in them which comes from sheer delight in the exercise of the imagination. They are plots which move with alacrity across landscapes which are decorated with a judicious eye for the unusual and the inventive.

In recent years the number of sf stories which are carefully serious in tone and treatment has increased considerably (somewhat to the annoyance of readers who only like its playful aspects). One reason for this is that sf has become popular with propagandists of various kinds. It has been taken up by feminists, who use possible futures both to display by exaggeration the iniquities of real-world sexual politics and to explore hypothetical societies whose sexual politics are very different. It has been taken up by conservationists and anti-nuclear campaigners who wish to offer dire and graphic warnings of the fates which might overtake the world if we are not more careful about polluting it in all the ways which are now possible. It has been taken up by libertarian expansionists eager to get on with the conquest of space, so that all the fetters of circumstance into which we are born might be eventually cast off. These campaigners have made sf very much more various than it used to be, and their conflicts of interest and purpose have served to sharpen up the arguments which they deploy against one another, and which they illustrate in the plotting of their stories.

There can be no doubt that the stories which we make up about possible futures have the power to affect the real attitudes which people have. We frequently hear people engaged in serious political argument referring to the imagery of *Nineteen Eighty-Four* and *Brave New World*. Popular ideas of the meaning and significance of the space programme have been very largely shaped by science fiction, and so have popular ideas about the environmental hazards and moral implications of genetic engineering and other bio-technologies. Whether sf has had a good or a bad effect on attitudes is open to argument, but it is undeniable that it is and will continue to be effective. It may well be the case that you want to write science fiction in order to express your feelings in respect of one or more of the causes listed above, and with some hope of adding to the effect which sf imagery has on the real attitudes of its readers. If so, then it may be as well to bear in mind that earnest anguish is not necessarily the most effective form of rhetoric.

It is a mistake for writers who wish to be entirely serious to neglect entirely the playful aspects of what they are doing. Nor should you simply think in terms of putting a sugar coat on a bitter pill, because that is the least subtle and most painfully inadequate way to approach the problem of blending amusement and instruction. There is a common way of talking which represents stories as things which might or might not have a message in them, but it is a foolish

79

way of talking. A story does not "have" or "contain" a message; a story *is* a kind of message, and whatever the message is saying can probably be said better if it is said elegantly, wittily, and with all due attention to the priorities of playfulness.

To sf writers whose ambition is to be purely playful I would offer the advice that they have chosen a very difficult path to take; to sf writers whose ambition is to be deadly serious I would offer the advice that they must beware lest they defeat their own purpose. I think that it is actually easier, as well as more rewarding, to set out with the object of combining the two. For the clever sf writer (perhaps aided by a convenient time-paradox) there should be no particular difficulty in having your cake and eating it too.

Chapter Eleven

The Economics of Science Fiction Writing

The rewards of sf writing can now be immense. Sf novels can get into the best-seller lists, the stars of the genre can command advances in the hundred thousand dollar range, and there are at least half a dozen people who have become millionaires by writing sf. On the other hand, there are hundreds of reasonably productive and fairly well-respected sf writers who do not make a living wage out of it and probably never will.

The economics of publishing is such that publishers spend large amounts of money buying and promoting a handful of favoured titles each year, while tens of thousands more titles are put out at what is effectively minimum cost (minimum cost meaning that the publisher will not only not advertise your book but will pay you as little for it as he can get away with). The reason why things work this way is not because publishers have formed a vile conspiracy to make a few fortunate writers rich while keeping the rest poor; to a large extent it simply reflects reading behaviour.

The great majority of "potential readers" read less than ten works of fiction per year, perhaps reading only when they are on trains or on holiday, and what they read is largely determined by current fashions – fashions which publishers try to influence as best they can by advertising, aided by such free advertising as book reviews in newspapers and published best-seller lists. That minority of readers who habitually read two or three works of fiction a week is subdivided into tinier minorities by virtue of the fact that many such readers are genre specialists. They provide relatively small but relatively safe inputs of money into the marketplace, supporting works which need no advertising at all to support them. In economic terms "literary fiction" may itself be regarded as a genre, but in most publishing of this kind formularization of the product (which is done very efficiently by publishers like Mills & Boon) is likely to be more effective as a marketing strategy than trying to improve literary quality.

Whole genres can undergo shifts in fashionability as the size of the loyal minorities which they serve varies, and individual writers can occasionally break out of their genre straitjackets to join the best-selling elite, but the logic of the situation insists that publishers should follow a policy of giving massive rewards to the few while being utterly miserly with the majority. In my more cynical moments, I have been known to suggest that in terms of economic theory, publishers stand in much the same relationship to writers as pimps to prostitutes or drug-smugglers to the peasants who grow opium poppies. In all three cases the result tends to be that the middlemen grow rich while the people who do the creative work don't. This is probably unfair to publishers, but all writers feel bitter about publishers occasionally.

The current word-rates for sf short stories are in the region of £30 per thousand. That is what *Interzone* pays in Britain, and approximately what *The Magazine of Science Fiction* pays in America. Flat word-rates have fallen out of fashion in America, where payments tend to vary with the length of the story and the prestige of the author; thus, for instance, *Analog* pays 6-8 cents per word up to 7,500 words, dropping to 5-6 cents for stories over 12,500, and 4 cents per word for serials. There are a couple of markets which pay much higher rates – the people who sell to *Omni* and *Playboy* can get as much as $2,000 for a short story – but they are, inevitably, the hardest markets to sell to.

It will be immediately obvious to anyone perusing these figures that there is no hope of making a living as a short story writer. A 6,000 word story will bring in something near to a (very moderate) week's wage, but the market is far too small to permit anyone to sell a story a week, or even a story a month. A story brilliant enough to catch the eye of the people who edit *Best SF of the Year* anthologies (of which there are currently three) might sell twice, or even three times, and there may be hope of it being further reprinted in years to come, but the sad fact is that short stories will never pay the rent.

Advances on royalties paid to sf writers are very variable, and not advertised in the same way that word-rates paid by magazines are, so my information about the current state of play is largely based on hearsay and personal experience, but should not be too far from the truth. In Britain £1,000 advances are commonplace for books which are to appear as original paperbacks, and a £5,000 advance would be regarded (by the publisher!) as large and very generous. In America $5,000 is probably the current standard for original paperbacks, though some publishers routinely try (and often get away with) offering as little as $2,500. Well-established authors with a good track record of sales probably have little difficulty getting $10,000 advances, but that would be unusual for a first novel.

This situation is complicated, of course, by the fact that a novel may well sell in Britain *and* America, so that it will bring in two advances. However, if the first publisher who buys the book buys world rights (which will usually be the case for authors who are not represented by agents) they will keep some of the advance (usually 20%) if and when they sublease rights to a publisher on the other side of the Atlantic.

Further complications arise if a novel is to be published in hardcover as well as in paperback. The advance paid by the hardcover publisher will cover both sets of rights, but will then be supplemented by a further sum when paperback rights are sub-leased. However, the hardcover publisher will keep up to 50% of the paperback advance, and will usually treat the rest as royalties to be set against the advance which he has already paid you. For this reason, the extra money which will be earned as a result of having two editions of the book may take some years to materialise.

Generally speaking, publishers adjust the advances which they pay writers according to the amount of royalties which they expect a book to earn. Sometimes they are wrong – either a book may fail by a wide margin to earn out its advance, or it may sell well enough to generate significant extra royalty revenue. In the former case the author gets to keep the unearned part of the advance, but may find the publisher more cautious when it is time to make a deal for another book. In the second case the author will get the extra money which the book earns, but not very quickly – he is unlikely to see it for at least a year after publication, and if the paperback does not appear until a year or eighteen months after the hardcover three years can easily pass between receipt of the advance (which will itself be paid half on signature of a contract and half on publication) and the first cheque for additional royalties.

If we cut through this Gordian knot of complications to take a crude example, it is not unlikely that a first sf novel in Britain might receive £1,500 advance for British paperback rights, later to be supplemented by 80% of $5,000 for US rights. The total earnings of the book might therefore be in the region of £4,000, which could be supplemented at some later stage by royalties and sums derived from the sale of translation rights, if the book proves successful. It will also earn a few pounds a year from Public Lending Right, provided that you take the trouble to register it. On this basis, a sf writer has to produce two books a year to live above the poverty-line, and it only requires one half-failure (a book which sells in one country but not the other) to make things difficult.

Many authors never get far beyond this level of advance, and there are professionals of long standing who have to reckon on producing at least two books a year to get by. There are professionals who do not even reach this stage, whose work appears in only one country – if it is Britain they may well have to churn out six or eight books a year to earn the same amount as a copy typist or a shop assistant.

In the past there has usually been a stratum of the market even lower than the general gamut of genre publishing, where the real hackwork is done, and where writers have to turn out a book a fortnight in order to get by. My good friend Lionel Fanthorpe produced nearly two hundred books in the late 1950s and early 1960s for John Spencer & Co., who paid the miserly sum of £22 10s. per volume; they never bothered with contracts and they proceeded to keep for themselves all sums earned by American editions and translations. Even in the year that he managed to produce 34 books he didn't earn enough to give up his regular job. There were still publishers buying in hackwork (including sf books) at £100 per book in the late 1970s, and though I know of no one paying such rates at the moment I would be very surprised if we had actually seen the last of this publishing Third World.

These figures serve to explain why I have always been anxious to avoid committing myself to full-time writing. As the amount of thought and effort invested in my books has increased their quality has improved, but the saleability of a novel depends at least as much on the state of the market as on its intrinsic merits, and when the boom which allowed me to get started was followed (as booms inevitably are) by a phase of contraction, better men than I found difficulty in keeping the wolf from the door.

I am presently employed as a university teacher. University teaching is the best profession to combine with writing because the vacations are so long. I have been doubly fortunate in landing such a job because I have been able to make the history of science fiction and other genres of fantastic fiction my main area of academic research, and have been able to make prolific contributions to the reference books which have sprung up to guide readers and librarians through the ever-expanding heritage of imaginative fiction. The word-rates for this kind of work are even worse than those for writing fiction – academic journals pay nothing, and it is not uncommon for reference-book contributors to be offered ten dollars per thousand words – but it has the advantage that one can reprocess the same information over and over again for different reference books.

Although I have become a reasonably hard-working writer, producing about four million words in the last twenty years and selling eighty per cent of them, my salary remains comfortably higher than my writing income. This experience leads me to suggest that would-be writers should not give up their day jobs unless they are (a) content to live dangerously close to the poverty line; (b) married to a highly-paid and very sympathetic spouse; or (c) already in possession of a huge offer for the paperback rights to their next book. For myself, I am living in hope that I might one day manage (c).

The economics of writing involve costs as well as income. At a minimal level, one can get by with paper and a typewriter, but a serious writer has expenses which go somewhat beyond that. Typescripts once prepared have to be mailed out, and the beginning writer has to face the probability that most of his stories will be rejected, mostly more than once. As Britain is so short of paying markets this will mean submission to American magazines, which is both expensive and time-consuming.

I always airmail my manuscripts, sending a photocopy of the story with a statement that it is NOT a simultaneous submission (editors don't like authors submitting their stories to more than one market at a time, and often won't read a story if they think an author might be doing that) and that it can be thrown away if rejected. I enclose with such submissions a self-addressed envelope with enough American stamps on it to carry back an airmail letter notifying me of failure or success. This saves time, but means that I have to bear the cost of making a new photocopy every time I submit a story. It also means that I need a way of getting hold of US stamps. The advantage of the system is that I usually learn what happens to the story in a matter of weeks.

A beginning writer cutting costs to the bone, who sends a story surface mail, enclosing sufficient International Reply Coupons to have it returned by the same method, must also add to the time it takes to travel the time it is likely to spend in the magazine's "slush pile". The slush pile is where editors put stories by people they have never heard of until they have a spare moment to look at them (or, more likely, until someone else can be persuaded to have a look at them). In my teens, when I was in this position, it usually took nine months to get a reply from America, and several manuscripts never came back at all. Even now, though American editors do pay me the compliment of not dumping my submissions in the slush pile, they very rarely buy a story from me, and it is diehard optimism rather than profits which leads me to make irregular submissions to them.

Another expense which most writers face is agents' fees. These can be partly avoided by not having an agent, and for beginning writers there is little point in trying to get one − it is just as hard for unknown writers to persuade a worthwhile agent to take them on as it is to persuade a worthwhile publisher – but the writer who sells world rights direct to a publisher must sign over a percentage of American and translation rights to pay for the publisher's subsequent agenting endeavours. A writer sufficiently established to need (and be able to get) a decent agent will have to pay at least 10% of domestic income and 15% of foreign income for the privilege. Successful agents nowadays try to hike this to 15% and 20%.

The writer who takes advantage of all the facilities which modern technology provides will also face considerable equipment costs. It is still possible to bash out stories on a second-hand manual typewriter, but a great deal of the hard work can be taken out of writing by using a word-processor. All the writers I know who use such machines regard them as a godsend – they eliminate the hassle involved in correcting errors with Tippex or strikeovers, and they make it possible to mess about with text as much as is necessary to get it into the required shape. Very few writers can produce a publishable first draft, and there never was a writer who couldn't improve on his first drafts. A word-processor allows you to alter your first draft as often as you like while producing it, and makes the job of editing it into a second, third or *n*th draft very much easier than retyping the whole thing.

The cheapest complete word-processing kit (the Amstrad 8256) sells as I write for about £400; a disc which will hold up to 40,000 words of text costs just under £3 and a cloth ribbon for the printer (similarly good for about 40,000 words before it gets grey enough to cause difficulties when photocopying) about £6. That same 40,000 words, printed in the double-spaced format required by publishers, will fill about 135 sheets of paper, which will cost about £1.35 to buy and about £6.75 to photocopy. It all mounts up.

The rewards and costs still missing from the economic equation cannot be quantified; they are the satisfactions and frustrations which one gets from being a writer. As everyone knows, writers are supposed to suffer terrible agonies for their art, but they are compensated by being better able to pretend to be superior human beings.

The benefits you will get in terms of other people thinking

well of you will probably be mixed. People are certainly impressed by the aura of creative power which a writer may wear, but can easily demolish it with a few well-chosen questions. Bob Shaw has observed that the deadliest questions usually come as a pair: "Have you published anything?" (loosely translated as: I've never heard of you) and "What name do you write under?" (loosely translatable as: I've definitely never heard of you).

Sf writers can, if they so wish, enjoy the advantages and disadvantages of more intimate contact with their audience by going to sf conventions; there they have at least a slim chance of bumping into people who have read their work, but must face the probability that these will be hardened convention-goers no longer awe-struck by the mere presence of a writer, who will be only too eager to tell you what you did wrong.

There is, however, an incomparable sweetness in hearing someone praise your work; you have to be a bit of an egomaniac to force yourself to write in the first place, and egomaniacs are the only people who really get a full measure of delight from the applause of others. Some very famous sf writers, because they are in regular touch with their fans, get almost as much opportunity to exercise and increase their egomania as people who appear in minor roles (weather forecasters and the like) on TV.

The two most difficult problems which the habitual writer has to cope with are book reviewers and spouses. Some lucky writers have trouble with neither: they get only good reviews, and turn out to have married one of those rare people who fully understand that when the writer is physically present but mentally absent he is only doing his job, and intends no personal insult. Most writers, though, will ultimately have to suffer the hideous torture of a cruel review, and the hard task of explaining to an injured spouse that you aren't *really* subjecting them to shameful and uncaring neglect – at least, not intentionally.

In order to cope with difficulties such as these I would strongly advise all would-be writers to cultivate a strong sense of self-respect. You do not have to believe that you are a genius, and if you do manage to convince yourself that you are a genius you will almost certainly be wrong. What you will need – and what any of us can produce if we really think hard enough about it and work hard to produce it – is some piece of work which you can turn to in your darkest hour, and of which you can honestly say: "I did that – *and nobody ever wrote anything like it before!*"

Chapter Twelve

Marketing your Science Fiction

Having rendered an account of the possible rewards to be gained from sf writing it is now necessary for me to offer a more detailed account of how to go about the business of making your way into the marketplace.

The first thing that must be said is that it is not necessary, and perhaps not even desirable, to begin submitting your manuscripts to professional outlets the moment you begin to produce them. Like everything else, writing takes practice, and it is entirely likely that you will have to do quite a bit of it before you begin to get near the standard of professional publishability.

Sf writers in this pre-professional phase do have advantages which many others do not have, in the shape of various amateur outlets. Sf has always had a fairly large, energetic and organised fan community, many of whose members go in for the production of amateur magazines, which are usually known as fanzines. Most fanzines are produced from stencils on cheap duplicators in print runs which rarely exceed a hundred. The ones which tend to be most long-lived are either "newszines" like David Langford's *Ansible* or fairly serious critical journals like the Australian *S F Commentary*, which are sufficiently useful or interesting to encourage a few people to pay for the privilege of receiving them. Mostly, fanzines are either given away free or swapped for other fanzines, and they exist principally as a medium for the editor to voice the opinions and publish the works of himself and a few friends. Fanzines which carry fiction are usually open for submissions, and provide an opportunity for beginning writers to expose their material to comment and criticism without actually having to pay for the privilege. Some fanzines with a larger-than-usual circulation or a particularly dedicated editor even pay very small word rates to contributors, thus becoming "semi-professional markets".

Because these fan magazines tend to appear irregularly, and frequently disappear forever, it is not worth my attempting to list the ones which currently exist. The best way for the beginning writer to find out about them is to join the British Science Fiction Association, which publicizes them in its own publications and harbours within its ranks groups of would-be writers who can easily get in touch with one another. Membership is currently £10 a year, and the present membership secretary is Joanne Raine, 33 Thornville Rd., Hartlepool, Cleveland TS26 8EW. As well as its critical journals *Vector* and *Paperback Inferno* the BSFA publishes a newszine called *Matrix* and a fanzine specifically aimed at would-be writers called *Focus*. There is also a British Fantasy Society, which would be equally useful for would-be fantasy and horror writers. It offers annual membership for £10, the current membership secretary being Di Wathen, 15 Stanley Rd., Morden, Surrey SM4 5DE.

I would strongly recommend beginning writers – especially younger ones – to explore these avenues before or as well as attempting to sell work to professional magazines. Contact with other people in the same situation as yourself can be invaluable in both practical and psychological terms. When I joined the BSFA in 1963 one of its internal organizations was a fanzine duplicating and distributing service, which gave access to a duplicator and bulk-mailing facilities. By joining that organization I was able to co-edit one fanzine and write for half a dozen others, and though it was all rather incestuous it did me the world of good in motivating me to produce work – not just stories but articles and book reviews. It gave me something solid to show for the work I did, and though a pile of duplicated fanzines whose average circulation was about 35 is not particularly wonderful in objective terms it is very much better than nothing.

Fanzine writing is sufficiently pleasurable, even in the absence of money, that I have never entirely stopped doing it; I rarely turn down requests from fanzine editors to supply material, though any stories which I write specially for them tend to be very short. My most recent fanzine piece appeared last year in *Out of the Woodwork*, a fanzine published by second-hand sf dealer Simon Gosden. Many sf writers feel the same way, and it is not at all unusual to find contributions donated by prestigious writers in fanzines.

The publications of the BSFA are not the only ones likely to be of interest and value to the would-be sf writer. There are two monthly newspapers published in America: *Locus* and *Science Fiction Chronicle*. Both began life as fanzines but as the field expanded so did the number of their readers and hence the number of their advertisers, enabling them to become commercially successful.

Locus, edited by Charlie Brown, is the larger of the two and has a circulation of several thousand, including the great majority of people professionally involved in the *genre*. It offers detailed listings of all sf, fantasy and horror books published in Britain and America, good review coverage of books and magazines, and all the news of the field, including regular coverage of the British scene by Mike Ashley. It produces occasional market reports for writers, including information about editors seeking submissions for anthologies of original stories. British subscriptions can be directed through Fantast (Medway) Ltd., P.O. Box 23, Upwell, Wisbech, Cambs. PE14 9BU. The current rate is $50 per year, the British equivalent varying with the exchange rate.

Science Fiction Chronicle, edited by Andy Porter, is smaller than *Locus*, but cheaper. It has a similar mix of features, including reports from Britain by Steve Jones and Jo Fletcher. The current rate for British subscriptions is £21 a year, and the British agent is Ethel Lindsay, 69 Barry Rd., Carnoustie, Angus DD7 7QQ.

Would-be sf writers should also take out a subscription to *Interzone*, which is likely to be the first paying market at which you aim your submissions. By the time this book appears the magazine will appear bimonthly instead of quarterly, so the subscription information shown in the latest issue available to me will then be out of date, but the address to which enquiries may be sent is 124 Osborne Rd., Brighton, BN1 6LU.

Beginning writers nowadays have other opportunities to meet their peers, and obtain advice. I know nothing about the correspondence courses which are widely advertised and can pass no judgment upon their usefulness, but I do have some slight experience of the kind of writing workshops and short courses which are often put on by various adult education organizations. It is also possible nowadays to go on week-long residential courses, where professional writers act as tutors, and though I have never taken part in one I have heard enthusiastic reports from one or two people who have.

There are a couple of specialized sf workshops run by groups of British writers, the most high-powered being the annual Milford workshop (held in Milford-on-Sea, Hants.) inspired by an American enterprise founded by Damon Knight in the 1950s, attendance at which is limited to professionals, by invitation only. You may be able to get access to one which is open to beginners. Participation in a workshop of this kind, in which all attendees must submit stories, and all must offer thoughtful criticism thereof, can be very useful, but I can testify from experience that it is not for the faint-hearted. Facing the critical judgments of a jury of one's peers can be harrowing, and the whole point of the system is to set aside the evasions of tact and politeness. Painful as it may prove, though, this kind of trial by ordeal is likely to do the ambitious writer more good than harm. If you can find one which meets regularly, within commuting distance of your home, it is well worth trying.

Writing courses offered as evening classes are not likely to run on this workshop principle, and will probably involve an appointed teacher passing (tactful) judgment on work submitted by attendees, with relatively little input from others. Such courses are very variable in quality, and their usefulness will usually depend on the attitude of the teacher. Some teachers of creative writing are likely to be hostile to sf, and some may even be hostile to the idea of writing any kind of commercial fiction. Beware of pretentious poets who live on their delusions of literary grandeur, and if you are ever unfortunate enough to end up in one of the worst kinds of "creative writing groups" (as you may easily do if you go to a British university to study English Literature) try to remember that the law of the land is not yet sufficiently enlightened to concede that the slaughter of literary snobs is justifiable homicide.

When the time comes to submit stories to people who

might pay for them, you must prepare a manuscript which is double-spaced and reasonably free of errors (though it is a good idea to correct typos and spelling-mistakes, even if it does ruin the perfection of your typescript). The first page of the story should include the title, the name to be used on the story, plus your real name if you are using a pseudonym, and your address. It should also display an approximate word count. Ever since a publisher lost the last page of one of my novels, and failed to notice that he had done so, I have been careful to put the page-count on the headsheet too, though this is not strictly necessary. If there is any scope for confusion you should also indicate what rights you are actually offering, though a sf magazine will probably make it clear to you if they respond positively what rights they are actually acquiring. *Interzone* sends out a detailed contract for every story it buys, though American magazines tend not to.

Beginning writers will probably have to market their first novels by submitting a complete text. Many writers, though, prefer to try and sell a novel in advance of writing the whole thing, on the basis of an outline and a few "sample chapters", or sometimes just an outline. Even first novelists can sometimes do this, provided they have some sort of a track record of short story sales which will serve to demonstrate their competence – award-winning short story writers may find publishers queueing up to offer an advance for their as-yet-unwritten novel, though the British BSFA award does not carry anything like the same publicity value as the American Hugo and Nebula Awards (which British writers hardly ever win).

The awful possibility of writing a novel which then fails to sell has made me an enthusiastic writer of outlines and sample chapters, but the failure to place an outline of a book you are keen to write is just as discouraging as failing to sell it when it is complete, and will almost certainly result in the book not being written. You have to bear in mind that if you write a book now and don't sell it, you can have another go in five years time, but the books that didn't sell in outline don't even exist.

I imagine that it is not too difficult for a writer to get trapped into the promiscuous production of parts of novels, only a few of which ever get completed. Had I been a full-time professional during these last seven or eight years I would probably have followed that route myself. That strategy could be effective in producing a regular supply of work, but it means that the writer is being controlled by the whims of editors, who are very likely to judge an outline according to whether it looks safely marketable. An editor may decide to take a risk with an unusual completed book because he has found it to be a satisfying thing to read, but commissioning a book on the basis of an outline is a stab in the dark, and it can hardly be solid enough to persuade him that a risk is worth taking. Writers who always want their contracts in advance are likely to find themselves confined to the production of conventional material, increasingly trying to shape their outlines to capture the fashions of the moment. You can make a living that way, but it might well take some of the joy and enterprise out of your writing.

As I commented in my brief autobiographical preface, the most important thing a writer needs is tenacity. There is a mythology of writing which speaks of talent and inspiration as if they were a kind of magical gift which you either have or don't have. It is true, alas, that we are not all equal when it comes to the natural fluency of our prose or the frequency with which good ideas occur to us, just as we are not all equal in speed and strength. But a "natural" ability to write will no more save a writer the trouble of working hard than innate strength will save a boxer the trouble of training. Only practice makes perfect, and most of us need a hell of a lot of practice just to be adequate.

The world is full of people who know they could write but never quite got around to it. There must be hundreds of millions of people in the world who once started to write a novel, but only tens of millions who got as far as half way, millions who finished it, and hundreds of thousands who then got stuck in again, having learned enough to do it better second time around. There are, alas, a few people in the world who have turned out novel after novel without ever selling one, but those few – who had the tenacity but not sufficient capacity for improvement to reach a saleable standard – are a very tiny minority. Most people, if they keep on long enough, get *somewhere* in the end.

There is another tiny minority, too, whose experiences set a valuable example to us all: those few writers whose works were rejected again and again and again by editors who would not take a chance on them, and yet in the end enjoyed a spectacular success. The most recent case I know of is Stephen R. Donaldson, whose *Chronicles of Thomas Covenant* were rejected forty times before being published, and then – without any kind of hype or advertisement – became runaway best-sellers. The editors who turned Donaldson down can point to a thousand other books they rejected which really *were* unsaleable, but the vital point to remember is that the swine who just sent your pearl of a story back with nothing but a coffee-stain and a printed rejection slip *can be wrong*. You cannot take it for granted that he *is* wrong, but you have an all-important margin of hope that might be enough to keep you going.

In my experience, the people who edit sf magazines and publish sf are friendlier than average. When I first started out I accumulated vast numbers of rejection slips, but some of them were actual letters with a few brief comments of encouragement. Most of the people who edit sf have been recruited from the sf community – if they are not writers they have at least been fans, and are more sympathetic to the hopes of people who send in unsolicited submissions than the editors of many other publications. The sheer pressure of time forces them to use form letters and printed rejection slips most of the time, but they present a more human face than many would-be writers find. Would-be sf writers who go to conventions can usually see their actual human faces too – a privilege rarely granted to hopeful writers in other fields.

Now that you have read this book from cover to cover, go write a science fiction story. In fact, write several. Do not lend this book to your best friend; tell him to buy his own, so that I will earn more royalties. On the other hand, if you borrowed it from the library, take it back immediately so that someone else can take it out, thereby adding a penny or so to my public lending right receipts. When you too are a published writer, you will realise how much these things mean to a chap.

I can honestly say by way of conclusion that I have rather

enjoyed writing this book, and that it has helped me to clarify things in my own mind in a way which may work to my future benefit. When I was in my teens I might have been too proud to take advice, but I am forty now and find it easier to listen. Nothing but good can come from thinking about better ways to write, and I hope that my signposts might have pointed you in directions where you can make discoveries of your own.

Make progress.